GIBSON SQUARE

This edition first published in 2005 by

Gibson Square Books Ltd
15 Gibson Square, London N1 0RD
Tel: +44 (0)20 7689 4790; Fax: +44 (0)20 7689 7395
publicity@gibsonsquare.com
www.gibsonsquare.com

UK & Ireland sales by Signature
20 Castlegate, York YO1 9RP
Tel 01904 633 633; Fax 01904 675 445
sales@signaturebooks.co.uk

UK & European distribution by Central Books Ltd
99 Wallis Road, UK London E9 5LN
Tel +44 (0)845 458 9911; Fax +44 (0)845 458 9912
info@centralbooks.com
www.centralbooks.com

Australian, New Zealand, Canada, South Africa, US sales,
please contact Gibson Square Books Ltd.

Acknowledgements; the publishers would like to thank Lewis H. Lapham for
special permission granted for this publication: 'Baghdad Year Zero' by Naomi
Klein Copyright © 2004 by *Harper's Magazine*. All rights reserved. Reproduced
from the September issue by special permission. 'Dying for Dollars' by Bryan
Mealer Copyright © 2004 Reproduced from the October issue by special per-
mission. 'A Puppet for All Seasons' Copyright © 2004 by *Harper's Magazine*.
All rights reserved. Reproduced from the December issue by special permission.
'The Terrorism to Come' by Walter Laqueur Copyright © 2004 by *Harper's
Magazine*. All rights reserved. Reproduced from the November issue
by special permission.

ISBN 1-903933-57-9

Printed by Bell & Bain Ltd., Glasgow

America's Real

Business in Iraq

Baghdad Year Zero

Naomi Klein

It was only after I had been in Baghdad for a month that I found
what I was looking for. I had traveled to Iraq a year after the war
began, at the height of what should have been a construction
boom, but after weeks of searching I had not seen a single piece
of heavy machinery apart from tanks and humvees. Then I saw it:
a construction crane. It was big and yellow and impressive, and
when I caught a glimpse of it around a corner in a busy shop-
ping district I thought that I was finally about to witness some
of the reconstruction I had heard so much about. But as I got
closer I noticed that the crane was not actually rebuilding anything—not one of the bombed-out government buildings that
still lay in rubble all over the city, nor one of the many power
lines that remained in twisted heaps even as the heat of summer
was starting to bear down. No, the crane was hoisting a giant
billboard to the top of a three-story building. SUNBULAH:
HONEY 100% NATURAL, made in Saudi Arabia.

Seeing the sign, I couldn't help but think about something

Senator John McCain had said back in October. Iraq, he said, is "a huge pot of honey that's attracting a lot of flies." The flies McCain was referring to were the Halliburtons and Bechtels, as well as the venture capitalists who flocked to Iraq in the path cleared by Bradley Fighting Vehicles and laser-guided bombs. The honey that drew them was not just no-bid contracts and Iraq's famed oil wealth but the myriad investment opportunities offered by a country that had just been cracked wide open after decades of being sealed off, first by the nationalist economic policies of Saddam Hussein, then by asphyxiating United Nations sanctions.

Looking at the honey billboard, I was also reminded of the most common explanation for what has gone wrong in Iraq, a complaint echoed by everyone from John Kerry to Pat Buchanan: Iraq is mired in blood and deprivation because George W. Bush didn't have "a postwar plan." The only problem with this theory is that it isn't true. The Bush Administration did have a plan for what it would do after the war; put simply, it was to lay out as much honey as possible, then sit back and wait for the flies.

The honey theory of Iraqi reconstruction stems from the most cherished belief of the war's ideological architects: that greed is good. Not good just for them and their friends but good for humanity, and certainly good for Iraqis. Greed creates profit, which creates growth, which creates jobs and products and services and everything else anyone could possibly need or want. The role of good government, then, is to create the optimal conditions for corporations to pursue their bottomless greed, so that they in turn can meet the needs of the society. The problem is that governments, even neoconservative governments, rarely get the chance to prove their sacred theory right: despite their enormous ideological advances, even George Bush's Republicans are, in their own minds, perennially sabotaged by meddling Democrats, intractable unions, and alarmist environmentalists.

Iraq was going to change all that. In one place on Earth, the theory would finally be put into practice in its most perfect and uncompromised form. A country of 25 million would not be rebuilt as it was before the war; it would be erased, disappeared. In its place would spring forth a gleaming showroom for laissez-faire economics, a utopia such as the world had never seen. Every policy that liberates multinational corporations to pursue their quest for profit would be put into place: a shrunken state, a flexible workforce, open borders, minimal taxes, no tariffs, no ownership restrictions. The people of Iraq would, of course, have to endure some short-term pain: assets, previously owned by the state, would have to be given up to create new opportunities for growth and investment. Jobs would have to be lost and, as foreign products flooded across the border, local businesses and family farms would, unfortunately, be unable to compete. But to the authors of this plan, these would be small prices to pay for the economic boom that would surely explode once the proper conditions were in place, a boom so powerful the country would practically rebuild itself.

The fact that the boom never came and Iraq continues to tremble under explosions of a very different sort should never be blamed on the absence of a plan. Rather, the blame rests with the plan itself, and the extraordinarily violent ideology upon which it is based.

* * *

Torturers believe that when electrical shocks are applied to various parts of the body simultaneously subjects are rendered so confused about where the pain is coming from that they become incapable of resistance. A declassified CIA "Counterintelligence Interrogation" manual from 1963 describes how a trauma inflicted on prisoners opens up "an interval—which may be extremely brief—of suspended animation, a kind of psychological shock or paralysis ... . [A]t this moment the source is far more open to suggestion, far likelier to comply." A similar theory applies to economic shock therapy, or "shock treatment," the ugly term used to describe the rapid implementation of free-market reforms imposed on Chile in the wake of General Augusto Pinochet's coup. The theory is that if painful economic "adjustments" are brought in rapidly and in the aftermath of a seismic social disruption like a war, a coup, or a government collapse, the population will be so stunned, and so preoccupied with the daily pressures of survival, that it too will go into suspended animation, unable to resist. As Pinochet's finance minister, Admiral Lorenzo Gotuzzo, declared, "The dog's tail must be cut off in one chop."

That, in essence, was the working thesis in Iraq, and in keeping with the belief that private companies are more suited than governments for virtually every task, the White House decided to privatize the task of privatizing Iraq's state-dominated economy. Two months before the war began, USAID began drafting a work order, to be handed out to a private company, to oversee Iraq's "transition to a sustainable market-driven economic system." The document states that the winning company (which turned out to be the KPMG offshoot Bearing Point) will take "appropriate advantage of the unique opportunity for rapid progress in this area presented by the current configuration of political circumstances." Which is precisely what happened.

L. Paul Bremer, who led the U.S. occupation of Iraq from May 2, 2003, until he caught an early flight out of Baghdad on June 28, admits that when he arrived, "Baghdad was on fire, literally, as I drove in from the airport." But before the fires from the "shock and awe" military onslaught were even extinguished, Bremer unleashed his shock therapy, pushing through more wrenching changes in one sweltering summer than the International Monetary Fund has managed to enact over three decades in Latin America. Joseph Stiglitz, Nobel laureate and former chief economist at the World Bank, describes Bremer's reforms as "an even more radical form of shock therapy than pursued in the former Soviet world."

The tone of Bremer's tenure was set with his first major act on the job: he fired 500,000 state workers, most of them soldiers, but also doctors, nurses, teachers, publishers, and printers. Next, he flung open the country's borders to absolutely unrestricted imports: no tariffs, no duties, no inspections, no taxes. Iraq, Bremer declared two weeks after he arrived, was "open for business."

One month later, Bremer unveiled the centrepiece of his reforms. Before the invasion, Iraq's non-oil-related economy had been dominated by 200 state-owned companies, which produced everything from cement to paper to washing machines. In June, Bremer flew to an economic summit in Jordan and announced that these firms would be privatized immediately. "Getting inefficient state enterprises into private hands," he said, "is essential for Iraq's economic recovery." It would be the largest state liquidation sale since the collapse of the Soviet Union.

But Bremer's economic engineering had only just begun. In September, to entice foreign investors to come to Iraq, he enacted a radical set of laws unprecedented in their generosity to multinational corporations. There was Order 37, which lowered Iraq's corporate tax rate from roughly 40 percent to a flat 15 percent. There was Order 39, which allowed foreign companies to own 100 percent of Iraqi assets outside of the natural-resource sector. Even better, investors could take 100 percent of the profits they made in Iraq out of the country; they would not be required to reinvest and they would not be taxed. Under Order 39, they could sign leases and contracts that would last for forty years. Order 40 welcomed foreign banks to Iraq under the same favorable terms. All that remained of Saddam Hussein's economic policies was a law restricting trade unions and collective bargaining.

If these policies sound familiar, it's because they are the same ones multinationals around the world lobby for from national governments and in international trade agreements. But while these reforms are only ever enacted in part, or in fits and starts, Bremer delivered them all, all at once. Overnight, Iraq went from being the most isolated country in the world to being, on paper, its widest-open market.

* * *

At first, the shock-therapy theory seemed to hold: Iraqis, reeling from violence both military and economic, were far too busy staying alive to mount a political response to Bremer's campaign. Worrying about the privatization of the sewage system was an unimaginable luxury with half the population lacking access to clean drinking water; the debate over the flat tax would have to wait until the lights were back on. Even in the international press, Bremer's new laws, though radical, were easily upstaged by more dramatic news of political chaos and rising crime.

Some people were paying attention, of course. That autumn was awash in "rebuilding Iraq" trade shows, in Washington, London, Madrid, and Amman. *The Economist* described Iraq under Bremer as "a capitalist dream," and a flurry of new consulting firms were launched promising to help companies get access to the Iraqi market, their boards of directors stacked with well-connected Republicans. The most prominent was New Bridge Strategies, started by Joe Allbaugh, former Bush-Cheney campaign manager. "Getting the rights to distribute Procter & Gamble products can be a gold mine," one of the company's partners enthused. "One well-stocked 7-Eleven could knock out thirty Iraqi stores; a Wal-Mart could take over the country."

Soon there were rumours that a McDonald's would be opening up in downtown Baghdad, funding was almost in place for a Starwood luxury hotel, and General Motors was planning to build an auto plant. On the financial side, HSBC would have branches all over the country, Citigroup was preparing to offer substantial loans guaranteed against future sales of Iraqi oil, and the bell was going to ring on a New York-style stock exchange in Baghdad any day.

In only a few months, the postwar plan to turn Iraq into a laboratory for the neocons had been realized. Leo Strauss may have provided the intellectual framework for invading Iraq pre-emptively, but it was that other University of Chicago professor, Milton Friedman, author of the anti-government manifesto *Capitalism and Freedom*, who supplied the manual for what to do once the country was safely in America's hands. This represented an enormous victory for the most ideological wing of the Bush Administration. But it was also something more: the culmination of two interlinked power struggles, one among Iraqi exiles advising the White House on its postwar strategy, the other within the White House itself.

As the British historian Dilip Hiro has shown, in *Secrets and Lies: Operation 'Iraqi Freedom' and After*, the Iraqi exiles pushing for the invasion were divided, broadly, into two camps. On one side were "the pragmatists," who favoured getting rid of Saddam and his immediate entourage, securing access to oil, and slowly introducing free-market reforms. Many of these exiles were part of the State Department's Future of Iraq Project, which generated a thirteen-volume report on how to restore basic services and transition to democracy after the war. On the other side was the "Year Zero" camp, those who believed that Iraq was so contaminated that it needed to be rubbed out and remade from scratch. The prime advocate of the pragmatic approach was Iyad Allawi, a former high-level Baathist who fell out with Saddam and started working for the CIA. The prime advocate of the Year Zero approach was Ahmad Chalabi, whose hatred of the Iraqi state for expropriating his family's assets during the 1958 revolution ran so deep he longed to see the entire country burned to the ground—everything, that is, but the Oil Ministry, which would be the nucleus of the new Iraq, the cluster of cells from which an entire nation would grow. He called this process "de-Baathification."

A parallel battle between pragmatists and true believers was being waged within the Bush Administration. The pragmatists were men like Secretary of State Colin Powell and General Jay Garner, the first U.S. envoy to postwar Iraq. General Garner's plan was straightforward enough: fix the infrastructure, hold quick and dirty elections, leave the shock therapy to the International Monetary Fund, and concentrate on securing U.S. military bases on the model of the Philippines. "I think we should look right now at Iraq as our coaling station in the Middle East," he told the BBC. He also paraphrased T. E. Lawrence, saying, "It's better for them to do it imperfectly than for us to do it for them perfectly." On the other side was the usual cast of neoconservatives: Vice President Dick Cheney, Secretary of Defense Donald Rumsfeld (who lauded Bremer's "sweeping reforms" as "some of the most enlightened and inviting tax and investment laws in the free world"), Deputy Secretary of Defense Paul Wolfowitz, and, perhaps most centrally, Undersecretary of Defense Douglas Feith. Whereas the State Department had its Future of Iraq report, the neocons had USAID's contract with Bearing Point to remake Iraq's economy: in 108 pages, "privatization" was mentioned no fewer than fifty-one times. To the true believers in the White House, General Garner's plans for postwar Iraq seemed hopelessly unambitious. Why settle for a mere coaling station when you can have a model free market? Why settle for the Philippines when you can have a beacon unto the world?

The Iraqi Year Zeroists made natural allies for the White House neoconservatives: Chalabi's seething hatred of the Baathist state fit nicely with the neocons' hatred of the state in general, and the two agendas effortlessly merged. Together, they came to imagine the invasion of Iraq as a kind of Rapture: where the rest of the world saw death, they saw birth—a country redeemed through violence, cleansed by fire. Iraq wasn't being destroyed by cruise missiles, cluster bombs, chaos, and looting; it was being born again. April 9, 2003, the day Baghdad fell, was Day One of Year Zero.

* * *

While the war was being waged, it still wasn't clear whether the pragmatists or the Year Zeroists would be handed control over occupied Iraq. But the speed with which the nation was conquered dramatically increased the neocons' political capital, since they had been predicting a "cakewalk" all along. Eight days after George Bush landed on that aircraft carrier under a banner that said MISSION ACCOMPLISHED, the President publicly signed on to the neocons' vision for Iraq to become a model corporate state that would open up the entire region. On May 9, Bush proposed the "establishment of a U.S.-Middle East free trade area within a decade"; three days later, Bush sent Paul

Bremer to Baghdad to replace Jay Garner, who had been on the job for only three weeks. The message was unequivocal: the pragmatists had lost; Iraq would belong to the believers.

A Reagan-era diplomat turned entrepreneur, Bremer had recently proven his ability to transform rubble into gold by waiting exactly one month after the September 11 attacks to launch Crisis Consulting Practice, a security company selling "terrorism risk insurance" to multinationals. Bremer had two lieutenants on the economic front: Thomas Foley and Michael Fleischer, the heads of "private sector development" for the Coalition Provisional Authority (CPA). Foley is a Greenwich, Connecticut, multimillionaire, a longtime friend of the Bush family and a Bush-Cheney campaign "pioneer" who has described Iraq as a modern California "gold rush." Fleischer, a venture capitalist, is the brother of former White House spokesman Ari Fleischer. Neither man had any high-level diplomatic experience and both use the term corporate "turnaround" specialist to describe what they do. According to Foley, this uniquely qualified them to manage Iraq's economy because it was "the mother of all turnarounds."

Many of the other CPA postings were equally ideological. The Green Zone, the city within a city that houses the occupation headquarters in Saddam's former palace, was filled with Young Republicans straight out of the Heritage Foundation, all of them given responsibility they could never have dreamed of receiving at home. Jay Hallen, a twenty-four-year-old who had applied for a job at the White House, was put in charge of launching Baghdad's new stock exchange. Scott Erwin, a twenty-one-year-old former intern to Dick Cheney, reported in an email home that "I am assisting Iraqis in the management of finances and budgeting for the domestic security forces." The college senior's favorite job before this one? "My time as an ice-cream truck driver." In those early days, the Green Zone felt a bit like the Peace Corps, for people who think the Peace Corps is a communist plot. It was a chance to sleep on cots, wear army boots, and cry "incoming"—all while being guarded around the clock by real soldiers.

The teams of KPMG accountants, investment bankers, think-tank lifers, and Young Republicans that populate the Green Zone have much in common with the IMF missions that rearrange the economies of developing countries from the presidential suites of Sheraton hotels the world over. Except for one rather significant difference: in Iraq they were not negotiating with the government to accept their "structural adjustments" in exchange for a loan; they were the government.

Some small steps were taken, however, to bring Iraq's U.S.-appointed politicians inside. Yegor Gaidar, the mastermind of Russia's mid-nineties privatization auction that gave away the country's assets to the reigning oligarchs, was invited to share his wisdom at a conference in Baghdad. Marek Belka, who as finance minister oversaw the same process in Poland, was brought in as well. The Iraqis who proved most gifted at mouthing the neocon lines were selected to act as what USAID calls local "policy champions"—men like Ahmad al Mukhtar, who told me of his countrymen, "They are lazy. The Iraqis by nature, they are very dependent.... They will have to depend on themselves, it is the only way to survive in the world today." Although he has no economics background and his last job was reading the English-language news on television, al Mukhtar was appointed director of foreign relations in the Ministry of Trade and is leading the charge for Iraq to join the World Trade Organization.

* * *

I had been following the economic front of the war for almost a year before I decided to go to Iraq. I attended the "Rebuilding Iraq" trade shows, studied Bremer's tax and investment laws, met with contractors at their home offices in the United States, interviewed the government officials in Washington who are making the policies. But as I prepared to travel to Iraq in March to see this experiment in free-market utopianism up close, it was becoming increasingly clear that all was not going according to plan. Bremer had been working on the theory that if you build a corporate utopia the corporations will come—but where were they? American multinationals were happy to accept U.S. tax-payer dollars to reconstruct the phone or electricity systems, but they weren't sinking their own money into Iraq. There was, as yet, no McDonald's or Wal-Mart in Baghdad, and even the sales of state factories, announced so confidently nine months earlier, had not materialized.

Some of the holdup had to do with the physical risks of doing business in Iraq. But there were other more significant risks as well. When Paul Bremer shredded Iraq's Baathist constitution and replaced it with what *The Economist* greeted approvingly as "the wish list of foreign investors," there was one small detail he failed to mention: It was all completely illegal.

The CPA derived its legal authority from United Nations Security Council Resolution 1483, passed in May 2003, which recognized the United States and Britain as Iraq's legitimate occupiers. It was this resolution that empowered Bremer to unilaterally make laws in Iraq. But the resolution also stated that the U.S. and Britain must "comply fully with their obligations under international law including in particular the Geneva Conventions of 1949 and the Hague Regulations of 1907." Both conventions were born as an attempt to curtail the unfortunate historical tendency among occupying powers to rewrite the rules so that they can economically strip the nations they control. With this in mind, the conventions stipulate that an occupier must abide by a country's existing laws unless "absolutely prevented" from doing so. They also state that an occupier does not own the "public buildings, real estate, forests and agricultural assets" of the country it is occupying but is rather their "administrator" and custodian, keeping them secure until sovereignty is reestablished. This was the true threat to the Year Zero plan: since America didn't own Iraq's assets, it could not legally sell them, which meant that after the occupation ended, an Iraqi government could come to power and decide that it wanted to keep the state companies in public hands, or, as is the norm in the Gulf region, to bar foreign firms from owning 100 percent of national assets. If that happened, investments made under Bremer's rules could be expropriated, leaving firms with no recourse because their investments had violated international law from the outset.

By November, trade lawyers started to advise their corporate clients not to go into Iraq just yet, that it would be better to wait until after the transition. Insurance companies were so spooked that not a single one of the big firms would insure investors for "political risk," that high-stakes area of insurance law that protects companies against foreign governments turning nationalist or socialist and expropriating their investments.

Even the U.S.-appointed Iraqi politicians, up to now so obedient, were getting nervous about their own political futures if they went along with the privatization plans. Communications Minister Haider al-Abadi told me about his first meeting with Bremer. "I said, 'Look, we don't have the mandate to sell any of this. Privatization is a big thing. We have to wait until there is an Iraqi government.'" Minister of Industry Mohamad Tofiq was even more direct: "I am not going to do something that is not legal, so that's it."

Both al-Abadi and Tofiq told me about a meeting—never reported in the press—that took place in late October 2003. At that gathering the twenty-five members of Iraq's Governing Council as well as the twenty-five interim ministers decided unanimously that they would not participate in the privatization of Iraq's state-owned companies or of its publicly owned infrastructure.

But Bremer didn't give up. International law prohibits occupiers from selling state assets themselves, but it doesn't say anything about the puppet governments they appoint. Originally, Bremer had pledged to hand over power to a directly elected Iraqi government, but in early November he went to Washington for a private meeting with President Bush and came back with a Plan B. On June 30 the occupation would officially end—but not really. It would be replaced by an appointed government, chosen by Washington. This government would not be bound by the international laws preventing occupiers from selling off state assets, but it would be bound by an "interim constitution," a document that would protect Bremer's investment and privatization laws.

The plan was risky. Bremer's June 30 deadline was awfully close, and it was chosen for a less than ideal reason: so that President Bush could trumpet the end of Iraq's occupation on the campaign trail. If everything went according to plan, Bremer would succeed in forcing a "sovereign" Iraqi government to carry out his illegal reforms. But if something went wrong, he would have to go ahead with the June 30 handover anyway because by then Karl Rove, and not Dick Cheney or Donald Rumsfeld, would be calling the shots. And if it came down to a choice between ideology in Iraq and the electability of George W. Bush, everyone knew which would win.

* * *

At first, Plan B seemed to be right on track. Bremer persuaded the Iraqi Governing Council to agree to everything: the new timetable, the interim government, and the interim constitution. He even managed to slip into the constitution a completely overlooked clause, Article 26. It stated that for the duration of the interim government, "The laws, regulations, orders and directives issued by the Coalition Provisional Authority ... shall remain in force" and could only be changed after general elections are held.

Bremer had found his legal loophole: There would be a window—seven months—when the occupation was officially over but before general elections were scheduled to take place. Within this window, the Hague and Geneva Conventions' bans on privatization would no longer apply, but Bremer's own laws, thanks to Article 26, would stand. During these seven months, foreign investors could come to Iraq and sign forty-year contracts to buy up Iraqi assets. If a future elected Iraqi government decided to change the rules, investors could sue for compensation.

But Bremer had a formidable opponent: Grand Ayatollah Ali al Sistani, the most senior Shia cleric in Iraq. al Sistani tried to block Bremer's plan at every turn, calling for immediate direct elections and for the constitution to be written after those elections, not before. Both demands, if met, would have closed Bremer's privatization window. Then, on March 2, with the Shia members of the Governing Council refusing to sign the interim constitution, five bombs exploded in front of mosques in Karbala and Baghdad, killing close to 200 worshipers. General John Abizaid, the top U.S. commander in Iraq, warned that the country was on the verge of civil war. Frightened by this prospect, al Sistani backed down and the Shia politicians signed the interim constitution. It was a familiar story: the shock of a violent attack paved the way for more shock therapy.

When I arrived in Iraq a week later, the economic project seemed to be back on track. All that remained for Bremer was to get his interim constitution ratified by a Security Council resolution, then the nervous lawyers and insurance brokers could relax and the sell-off of Iraq could finally begin. The CPA, meanwhile, had launched a major new P.R. offensive designed to reassure investors that Iraq was still a safe and exciting place to do business. The centrepiece of the campaign was Destination Baghdad Exposition, a massive trade show for potential investors to be held in early April at the Baghdad International Fairgrounds. It was the first such event inside Iraq, and the organizers had branded the trade fair "DBX," as if it were some sort of Mountain Dew–sponsored dirt-bike race. In keeping with the extreme-sports theme, Thomas Foley traveled to Washington to tell a gathering of executives that the risks in Iraq are akin "to skydiving or riding a motorcycle, which are, to many, very acceptable risks."

But three hours after my arrival in Baghdad, I was finding these reassurances extremely hard to believe. I had not yet unpacked when my hotel room was filled with debris and the windows in the lobby were shattered. Down the street, the Mount Lebanon Hotel had just been bombed, at that point the largest attack of its kind since the official end of the war. The next day, another hotel was bombed in Basra, then two Finnish businessmen were murdered on their way to a meeting in Baghdad. Brigadier General Mark Kimmitt finally admitted that there was a pattern at work: "the extremists have started shifting away from the hard targets … [and] are now going out of their way to specifically target softer targets." The next day, the State Department updated its travel advisory: U.S. citizens were "strongly warned against travel to Iraq."

The physical risks of doing business in Iraq seemed to be spiraling out of control. This, once again, was not part of the original plan. When Bremer first arrived in Baghdad, the armed resistance was so low that he was able to walk the streets with a minimal security entourage. During his first four months on the job, 109 U.S. soldiers were killed and 570 were wounded. In the following four months, when Bremer's shock therapy had taken effect, the number of U.S. casualties almost doubled, with 195 soldiers killed and 1,633 wounded. There are many in Iraq who argue that these events are connected—that Bremer's reforms were the single largest factor leading to the rise of armed resistance.

Take, for instance, Bremer's first casualties. The soldiers and workers he laid off without pensions or severance pay didn't all disappear quietly. Many of them went straight into the mujahedeen, forming the backbone of the armed resistance. "Half a million people are now worse off, and there you have the water tap that keeps the insurgency going. It's alternative employment," says Hussain Kubba, head of the prominent Iraqi business group Kubba Consulting. Some of Bremer's other economic casualties also have failed to go quietly. It turns out that many of the businessmen whose companies are threatened by Bremer's investment laws have decided to make investments of their own—in the resistance. It is partly their money that keeps fighters in Kalashnikovs and RPGs.

These developments present a challenge to the basic logic of shock therapy: the neocons were convinced that if they brought in their reforms quickly and ruthlessly, Iraqis would be too stunned to resist. But the shock appears to have had the opposite effect; rather than the predicted paralysis, it jolted many Iraqis into action, much of it extreme. Haider al-Abadi, Iraq's minister of communication, puts it this way: "We know that there are terrorists in the country, but previously they were not successful, they were isolated. Now because the whole country is unhappy, and a lot of people don't have jobs ... these terrorists are finding listening ears."

Bremer was now at odds not only with the Iraqis who opposed his plans but with U.S military commanders charged with putting down the insurgency his policies were feeding. Heretical questions began to be raised: instead of laying people off, what if the CPA actually created jobs for Iraqis? And instead of rushing to sell off Iraq's 200 state-owned firms, how about putting them back to work?

* * *

From the start, the neocons running Iraq had shown nothing but disdain for Iraq's state-owned companies. In keeping with their Year Zero-apocalyptic glee, when looters descended on the factories during the war, U.S. forces did nothing. Sabah Asaad, managing director of a refrigerator factory outside Baghdad, told me that while the looting was going on, he went to a nearby U.S. Army base and begged for help. "I asked one of the officers to send two soldiers and a vehicle to help me kick out the looters. I was crying. The officer said, 'Sorry, we can't do anything, we need an order from President Bush.'" Back in Washington, Donald Rumsfeld shrugged. "Free people are free to make mistakes and commit crimes and do bad things."

To see the remains of Asaad's football-field-size warehouse is to understand why Frank Gehry had an artistic crisis after September 11 and was briefly unable to design structures resembling the rubble of modern buildings. Asaad's looted and burned factory looks remarkably like a heavy-metal version of Gehry's Guggenheim in Bilbao, Spain, with waves of steel, buckled by fire, lying in terrifyingly beautiful golden heaps. Yet all was not lost. "The looters were good-hearted," one of Asaad's painters told me, explaining that they left the tools and machines behind, "so we could work again." Because the machines are still there, many factory managers in Iraq say that it would take little for them to return to full production. They need emergency generators to cope with daily blackouts, and they need capital for parts and raw materials. If that happened, it would have tremendous implications for Iraq's stalled reconstruction, because it would mean that many of the key materials needed to rebuild—cement and steel, bricks and furniture—could be produced inside the country.

But it hasn't happened. Immediately after the nominal end of the war, Congress appropriated $2.5 billion for the reconstruction of Iraq, followed by an additional $18.4 billion in October. Yet as of July 2004, Iraq's state-owned factories had been pointedly excluded from the reconstruction contracts. Instead, the billions have all gone to Western companies, with most of the materials for the reconstruction imported at great expense from abroad.

With unemployment as high as 67 percent, the imported products and foreign workers flooding across the borders have become a source of tremendous resentment in Iraq and yet another open tap fueling the insurgency. And Iraqis don't have to look far for reminders of this injustice; it's on display in the most ubiquitous symbol of the occupation: the blast wall. The ten-foot-high slabs of reinforced concrete are everywhere in

Iraq, separating the protected—the people in upscale hotels, luxury homes, military bases, and, of course, the Green Zone— from the unprotected and exposed. If that wasn't injury enough, all the blast walls are imported, from Kurdistan, Turkey, or even farther afield, this despite the fact that Iraq was once a major manufacturer of cement, and could easily be again. There are seventeen state-owned cement factories across the country, but most are idle or working at only half capacity. According to the Ministry of Industry, not one of these factories has received a single contract to help with the reconstruction, even though they could produce the walls and meet other needs for cement at a greatly reduced cost. The CPA pays up to $1,000 per imported blast wall; local manufacturers say they could make them for $100. Minister Tofiq says there is a simple reason why the Americans refuse to help get Iraq's cement factories running again: among those making the decisions, "no one believes in the public sector."[1]

This kind of ideological blindness has turned Iraq's occupiers into prisoners of their own policies, hiding behind walls that, by their very existence, fuel the rage at the U.S. presence, thereby feeding the need for more walls. In Baghdad the concrete barriers have been given a popular nickname: Bremer Walls.

As the insurgency grew, it soon became clear that if Bremer went ahead with his plans to sell off the state companies, it could worsen the violence. There was no question that privati-

---

[1] Tofiq did say that several U.S. companies had expressed strong interest in buying the state-owned cement factories. This supports a widely held belief in Iraq that there is a deliberate strategy to neglect the state firms so that they can be sold more cheaply—a practice known as "starve then sell."

zation would require layoffs: the Ministry of Industry estimates that roughly 145,000 workers would have to be fired to make the firms desirable to investors, with each of those workers supporting, on average, five family members. For Iraq's besieged occupiers the question was: Would these shock-therapy casualties accept their fate or would they rebel?

*   *   *

The answer arrived, in rather dramatic fashion, at one of the largest state-owned companies, the General Company for Vegetable Oils. The complex of six factories in a Baghdad industrial zone produces cooking oil, hand soap, laundry detergent, shaving cream, and shampoo. At least that is what I was told by a receptionist who gave me glossy brochures and calendars boasting of "modern instruments" and "the latest and most up to date developments in the field of industry." But when I approached the soap factory, I discovered a group of workers sleeping outside a darkened building. Our guide rushed ahead, shouting something to a woman in a white lab coat, and suddenly the factory scrambled into activity: lights switched on, motors revved up, and workers—still blinking off sleep—began filling two-liter plastic bottles with pale blue Zahi brand dishwashing liquid.

I asked Nada Ahmed, the woman in the white coat, why the factory wasn't working a few minutes before. She explained that they have only enough electricity and materials to run the machines for a couple of hours a day, but when guests arrive— would-be investors, ministry officials, journalists—they get them going. "For show," she explained. Behind us, a dozen bulky machines sat idle, covered in sheets of dusty plastic and secured with duct tape.

In one dark corner of the plant, we came across an old man hunched over a sack filled with white plastic caps. With a thin metal blade lodged in a wedge of wax, he carefully whittled down the edges of each cap, leaving a pile of shavings at his feet. "We don't have the spare part for the proper mold, so we have to cut them by hand," his supervisor explained apologetically. "We haven't received any parts from Germany since the sanctions began." I noticed that even on the assembly lines that were nominally working there was almost no mechanization: bottles were held under spouts by hand because conveyor belts don't convey, lids once snapped on by machines were being hammered in place with wooden mallets. Even the water for the factory was drawn from an outdoor well, hoisted by hand, and carried inside.

The solution proposed by the U.S. occupiers was not to fix the plant but to sell it, and so when Bremer announced the privatization auction back in June 2003 this was among the first companies mentioned. Yet when I visited the factory in March, nobody wanted to talk about the privatization plan; the mere mention of the word inside the plant inspired awkward silences and meaningful glances. This seemed an unnatural amount of subtext for a soap factory, and I tried to get to the bottom of it when I interviewed the assistant manager. But the interview itself was equally odd: I had spent half a week setting it up, submitting written questions for approval, getting a signed letter of permission from the minister of industry, being questioned and searched several times. But when I finally began the interview, the assistant manager refused to tell me his name or let me record the conversation. "Any manager mentioned in the press is attacked afterwards," he said. And when I asked whether the company was being sold, he gave this oblique response: "If the decision was up to the workers, they are against privatization; but if it's up to the high-ranking officials and government, then privatization is an order and orders must be followed."

I left the plant feeling that I knew less than when I'd arrived. But on the way out of the gates, a young security guard handed my translator a note. He wanted us to meet him after work at a nearby restaurant, "to find out what is really going on with privatization." His name was Mahmud, and he was a twenty-five-year-old with a neat beard and big black eyes. (For his safety, I have omitted his last name.) His story began in July, a few weeks after Bremer's privatization announcement. The company's manager, on his way to work, was shot to death. Press reports speculated that the manager was murdered because he was in favour of privatizing the plant, but Mahmud was convinced that he was killed because he opposed the plan. "He would never have sold the factories like the Americans want. That's why they killed him."

The dead man was replaced by a new manager, Mudhfar Ja'far. Shortly after taking over, Ja'far called a meeting with ministry officials to discuss selling off the soap factory, which would involve laying off two thirds of its employees. Guarding that meeting were several security officers from the plant. They listened closely to Ja'far's plans and promptly reported the alarming news to their coworkers. "We were shocked," Mahmud recalled. "If the private sector buys our company, the first thing they would do is reduce the staff to make more money. And we will be forced into a very hard destiny, because the factory is our only way of living."

Frightened by this prospect, a group of seventeen workers, including Mahmud, marched into Ja'far's office to confront him on what they had heard. "Unfortunately, he wasn't there, only the assistant manager, the one you met," Mahmud told me. A fight broke out: one worker struck the assistant manager, and a bodyguard fired three shots at the workers. The crowd then attacked the bodyguard, took his gun, and, Mahmud said, "stabbed him with a knife in the back three times. He spent a month in the hospital." In January there was even more violence. On their way to work, Ja'far, the manager, and his son were shot and badly injured. Mahmud told me he had no idea who was behind the attack, but I was starting to understand why factory managers in Iraq try to keep a low profile.

At the end of our meeting, I asked Mahmud what would happen if the plant was sold despite the workers' objections. "There are two choices," he said, looking me in the eye and smiling kindly. "Either we will set the factory on fire and let the flames devour it to the ground, or we will blow ourselves up inside of it. But it will not be privatized."

If there ever was a moment when Iraqis were too disoriented to resist shock therapy, that moment has definitely passed. Labor relations, like everything else in Iraq, has become a blood sport. The violence on the streets howls at the gates of the factories, threatening to engulf them. Workers fear job loss as a death sentence, and managers, in turn, fear their workers, a fact that makes privatization distinctly more complicated than the neocons foresaw.[2]

* * *

As I left the meeting with Mahmud, I got word that there was a major demonstration outside the CPA headquarters. Supporters of the radical young cleric Moqtada al Sadr were protesting the closing of their newspaper, *al Hawza*, by military police. The CPA accused *al Hawza* of publishing "false articles" that could "pose the real threat of violence." As an example, it cited an article that claimed Bremer "is pursuing a policy of starving the Iraqi people to make them preoccupied with procuring their daily bread so they do not have the chance to demand their political and individual freedoms." To me it sounded less like hate literature than a concise summary of Milton Friedman's recipe for shock therapy.

A few days before the newspaper was shut down, I had gone to Kufa during Friday prayers to listen to al Sadr at his mosque. He had launched into a tirade against Bremer's newly signed interim constitution, calling it "an unjust, terrorist document." The message of the sermon was clear: Grand Ayatollah Ali al Sistani may have backed down on the constitution, but al Sadr and his supporters were still determined to fight it—and if they succeeded they would sabotage the neocons' careful plan to

---

[2]   It is in Basra where the connections between economic reforms and the rise of the resistance was put in starkest terms. In December the union representing oil workers was negotiating with the Oil Ministry for a salary increase. Getting nowhere, the workers offered the ministry a simple choice: increase their paltry salaries or they would all join the armed resistance. They received a substantial raise.

saddle Iraq's next government with their "wish list" of laws. With the closing of the newspaper, Bremer was giving al Sadr his response: he wasn't negotiating with this young upstart; he'd rather take him out with force.

When I arrived at the demonstration, the streets were filled with men dressed in black, the soon-to-be legendary Mahdi Army. It struck me that if Mahmud lost his security guard job at the soap factory, he could be one of them. That's who al Sadr's foot soldiers are: the young men who have been shut out of the neocons' grand plans for Iraq, who see no possibilities for work, and whose neighbourhoods have seen none of the promised reconstruction. Bremer has failed these young men, and everywhere that he has failed, Moqtada al Sadr has cannily set out to succeed. In Shia slums from Baghdad to Basra, a network of Sadr Centers coordinate a kind of shadow reconstruction. Funded through donations, the centres dispatch electricians to fix power and phone lines, organize local garbage collection, set up emergency generators, run blood drives, direct traffic where the streetlights don't work. And yes, they organize militias too. Al Sadr took Bremer's economic casualties, dressed them in black, and gave them rusty Kalashnikovs. His militiamen protected the mosques and the state factories when the occupation authorities did not, but in some areas they also went further, zealously enforcing Islamic law by torching liquor stores and terrorizing women without the veil. Indeed, the astronomical rise of the brand of religious fundamentalism that al Sadr represents is another kind of blowback from Bremer's shock therapy: if the reconstruction had provided jobs, security, and services to Iraqis, al Sadr would have been deprived of both his mission and many of his newfound followers.

At the same time as al Sadr's followers were shouting "Down with America" outside the Green Zone, something was happening in another part of the country that would change everything. Four American mercenary soldiers were killed in Fallujah, their charred and dismembered bodies hung like trophies over the Euphrates. The attacks would prove a devastating blow for the neocons, one from which they would never recover. With these images, investing in Iraq suddenly didn't look anything like a capitalist dream; it looked like a macabre nightmare made real.

The day I left Baghdad was the worst yet. Fallujah was under siege and Brig. Gen. Kimmitt was threatening to "destroy the al-Mahdi Army." By the end, roughly 2,000 Iraqis were killed in these twin campaigns. I was dropped off at a security checkpoint several miles from the airport, then loaded onto a bus jammed with contractors lugging hastily packed bags. Although no one was calling it one, this was an evacuation: over the next week 1,500 contractors left Iraq, and some governments began airlifting their citizens out of the country. On the bus no one spoke; we all just listened to the mortar fire, craning our necks to see the red glow. A guy carrying a KPMG briefcase decided to lighten things up. "So is there business class on this flight?" he asked the silent bus. From the back, somebody called out, "Not yet."

Indeed, it may be quite a while before business class truly arrives in Iraq. When we landed in Amman, we learned that we had gotten out just in time. That morning three Japanese civilians were kidnapped and their captors were threatening to burn them alive. Two days later Nicholas Berg went missing and was not seen again until the snuff film surfaced of his beheading, an even more terrifying message for U.S. contractors than the charred bodies in Fallujah. These were the start of a wave of kidnappings and killings of foreigners, most of them businesspeople, from a rainbow of nations: South Korea, Italy, China, Nepal, Pakistan, the Philippines, Turkey. By the end of June more than ninety contractors were reported dead in Iraq. When seven Turkish contractors were kidnapped in June, their captors asked the "company to cancel all contracts and pull out employees from Iraq." Many insurance companies stopped selling life insurance to contractors, and others began to charge premiums as high as $10,000 a week for a single Western executive—the same price some insurgents reportedly pay for a dead American.

For their part, the organizers of DBX, the historic Baghdad trade fair, decided to relocate to the lovely tourist city of Diyarbakir in Turkey, "just 250 km from the Iraqi border." An Iraqi landscape, only without those frightening Iraqis. Three weeks later just fifteen people showed up for a Commerce Department conference in Lansing, Michigan, on investing in Iraq. Its host, Republican Congressman Mike Rogers, tried to reassure his skeptical audience by saying that Iraq is "like a rough neighbourhood anywhere in America." The foreign investors, the ones who were offered every imaginable free-market enticement, are clearly not convinced; there is still no sign of them. Keith Crane, a senior economist at the Rand Corporation who has worked for the CPA, put it bluntly: "I don't believe the board of a multinational company could approve a major investment in this environment. If people are shooting at each other, it's just difficult to do business." Hamid Jassim Khamis, the manager of the largest soft-drink bottling plant in the region, told me he can't find any investors, even though he landed the exclusive rights to produce Pepsi in central Iraq. "A lot of people have approached us to invest in the factory, but people are really hesitating now." Khamis said he couldn't blame them; in five months he has survived an attempted assassination, a carjacking, two bombs planted at the entrance of his factory, and the kidnapping of his son.

Despite having been granted the first license for a foreign bank to operate in Iraq in forty years, HSBC still hasn't opened any branches, a decision that may mean losing the coveted license altogether. Procter & Gamble has put its joint venture on hold, and so has General Motors. The U.S. financial backers of the Starwood luxury hotel and multiplex have gotten cold feet, and Siemens AG has pulled most staff from Iraq. The bell hasn't rung yet at the Baghdad Stock Exchange—in fact you can't even use credit cards in Iraq's cash-only economy. New Bridge Strategies, the company that had gushed back in October about how "a Wal-Mart could take over the country," is sounding distinctly humbled. "McDonald's is not opening anytime soon," company partner Ed Rogers told the *Washington Post.* Neither is Wal-Mart. The *Financial Times* has declared Iraq "the most dangerous place in the world in which to do business." It's quite an accomplishment: in trying to design the best place in the world to do business, the neocons have managed to create the worst, the most eloquent indictment yet of the guiding logic behind deregulated free markets.

The violence has not just kept investors out; it also forced Bremer, before he left, to abandon many of his central economic policies. Privatization of the state companies is off the table;

instead, several of the state companies have been offered up for lease, but only if the investor agrees not to lay off a single employee. Thousands of the state workers that Bremer fired have been rehired, and significant raises have been handed out in the public sector as a whole. Plans to do away with the food-ration program have also been scrapped—it just doesn't seem like a good time to deny millions of Iraqis the only nutrition on which they can depend.

*   *   *

The final blow to the neocon dream came in the weeks before the handover. The White House and the CPA were rushing to get the U.N. Security Council to pass a resolution endorsing their handover plan. They had twisted arms to give the top job to for-mer CIA agent Iyad Allawi, a move that will ensure that Iraq becomes, at the very least, the coaling station for U.S. troops that Jay Garner originally envisioned. But if major corporate investors were going to come to Iraq in the future, they would need a stronger guarantee that Bremer's economic laws would stick. There was only one way of doing that: the Security Council resolution had to ratify the interim constitution, which locked in Bremer's laws for the duration of the interim government. But al Sistani once again objected, this time unequivocally, saying that the constitution has been "rejected by the majority of the Iraqi people." On June 8 the Security Council unanimously passed a resolution that endorsed the handover plan but made absolute-ly no reference to the constitution. In the face of this far-reach-ing defeat, George W. Bush celebrated the resolution as a historic victory, one that came just in time for an election trail photo op at the G-8 Summit in Georgia.

With Bremer's laws in limbo, Iraqi ministers are already talking openly about breaking contracts signed by the CPA. Citigroup's loan scheme has been rejected as a misuse of Iraq's oil revenues. Iraq's communication minister is threatening to renegotiate contracts with the three communications firms providing the country with its disastrously poor cell phone service. And the Lebanese and U.S. companies hired to run the state television network have been informed that they could lose their licenses because they are not Iraqi. "We will see if we can change the contract," Hamid al-Kifaey, spokesperson for the Governing Council, said in May. "They have no idea about Iraq." For most investors, this complete lack of legal certainty simply makes Iraq too great a risk.

But while the Iraqi resistance has managed to scare off the first wave of corporate raiders, there's little doubt that they will return. Whatever form the next Iraqi government takes—nationalist, Islamist, or free market—it will inherit a shattered nation with a crushing $120 billion debt. Then, as in all poor countries around the world, men in dark blue suits from the IMF will appear at the door, bearing loans and promises of economic boom, provided that certain structural adjustments are made, which will, of course, be rather painful at first but well worth the sacrifice in the end. In fact, the process has already begun: the IMF is poised to approve loans worth $2.5–$4.25 billion, pending agreement on the conditions. After an endless succession of courageous last stands and far too many lost lives, Iraq will become a poor nation like any other, with politicians determined to introduce policies rejected by the vast majority of the population, and all the imperfect compromises that will entail. The free market will no doubt come to Iraq, but the neoconservative dream of transforming the country into a free-market utopia has already died.

The great historical irony of the catastrophe unfolding in Iraq is that the shock-therapy reforms that were supposed to create an economic boom that would rebuild the country have instead fueled a resistance that ultimately made reconstruction impossible. Bremer's reforms unleashed forces that the neocons neither predicted nor could hope to control, from armed insurrections inside factories to tens of thousands of unemployed young men arming themselves. These forces have transformed Year Zero in Iraq into the mirror opposite of what the neocons envisioned: not a corporate utopia but a ghoulish dystopia, where going to a simple business meeting can get you lynched, burned alive, or beheaded. These dangers are so great that in Iraq global capitalism has retreated, at least for now. For the neocons, this must be a shocking development: their ideological belief in greed turns out to be stronger than greed itself.

Iraq was to the neocons what Afghanistan was to the Taliban: the one place on Earth where they could force everyone to live by the most literal, unyielding interpretation of their sacred texts. One would think that the bloody results of this experiment would inspire a crisis of faith: in the country where they had absolute free reign, where there was no local government to blame, where economic reforms were introduced at their most shocking and most perfect, they created, instead of a model free market, a failed state no right-thinking investor would touch.

And yet the Green Zone neocons and their masters in Washington are no more likely to reexamine their core beliefs than the Taliban mullahs were inclined to search their souls when their Islamic state slid into a debauched Hades of opium and sex slavery. When facts threaten true believers, they simply close their eyes and pray harder.

Which is precisely what Thomas Foley has been doing. The former head of "private sector development" has left Iraq, a country he had described as "the mother of all turnarounds." On April 30 in Washington he addressed a crowd of entrepreneurs about business prospects in Baghdad. It was a tough day to be giving an upbeat speech: that morning the first photographs had appeared out of Abu Ghraib, including one of a hooded prisoner with electrical wires attached to his hands. This was another kind of shock therapy, far more literal than the one Foley had helped to administer, but not entirely unconnected. "Whatever you're seeing, it's not as bad as it appears," Foley told the crowd. "You just need to accept that on faith."

Naomi Klein is the author of *No Logo* (2000) and *Fences and Windows* (2002), as well as writer/producer of *The Take*, a new documentary on Argentina's occupied factories.

Dying for Dollars

Bryan Mealer

The man from the Army takes the stage of the Emperors Ballroom and scans the faces of the potential recruits. Three hundred pairs of eyes stare back, hungry and eager to know. We sit behind rows of conference tables, sipping coffee out of paper cups. The overhead chandeliers bathe us in a golden light. The Army man sees a room of empty holes waiting to be filled.

It's early June 2004 at Caesars Palace, in Las Vegas, and the government is getting us up to speed on how to participate in the glorious rebuilding of Iraq. It's one of many stops on a worldwide tour, in which bureaucratic evangelists from the Commerce Department and the U.S. Army spread the good news about what Uncle Sam is doing in the Babylonian desert and the myriad ways in which the Coalition is dishing out $18.4 billion in reconstruction funds to good folks like you and me.

The Vegas conference, located on the fourth floor of the Palace Tower, is hosted by the Army Small Business Office, and it has attracted several hundred business owners from every industry. Executives from Halliburton, Parsons Corporation, Perini Corporation, Lucent Technologies, Contrack International, FluorAMEC, and Washington Group International—some of the major "prime" contractors currently working in Iraq—will give elaborate presentations on how to compete for multimillion-dollar subcontracts with their companies. There are slide shows and Q&As throughout the day and, at night, dancing girls in the Shadow Bar and 3-for-1 slots.

The man from the Army is Mark Lumer, chief of civilian contracts, and he flew all night just to explain the real story in Iraq. Lumer's gray beard is wild and his suit swallows him like a fish, but his eyes are sharp and probe the mettle in our souls. Where there are dark patches of ignorance and doubt, Lumer replaces them with the Truth and the Way. All we have to do is listen and believe. The story goes something like this:

> *Right now it is a new day in Iraq. Right now, friends, Iraq is being delivered from twenty-five years of slavery. Iraq is an infant and we are teaching it how to walk. History will not judge us as mere occupiers but as compassionate liberators and good Samaritans, swift merchants of hope and the rule of law. Right now in Iraq, America is in the Quality of Life business. The American people have given Iraq a gift of $18.4 billion to rebuild the highways, hospitals, electricity grid, communications networks, law and justice systems, as well as provide clean drinking water and a modern oil infrastructure. Why, you ask, should we rebuild Iraq? Because it's the right thing to do. Because an Iraq that is peaceful and prosperous will no longer pose a threat to its neigh-*

bours, to the region, and to America. An Iraq that is peaceful will make money, and when people make money, they no longer want to kill you.

Lumer says Congress has ensured that a portion of the reconstruction money will go to American small businesses, which have already won more than $500 million in contracts, and that's just the beginning. American prime contractors and their subs are currently rebuilding military bases, hydroelectric plants, transmission towers, along with scores of other projects. But since the government is in the business of helping Iraq help itself, he says, 77 percent of the contracts have gone to Iraqi firms.

The work we're doing is historic in scale. In a matter of months, he says, Iraq will have over 6,000 megawatts of electricity. Sewage and water lines will exist in every major city for the first time in its 6,000-year history. America, he says, has renovated 1,500 schools, hundreds of hospitals, and enabled over 400,000 people to have telephones in their homes. America has already put new textbooks in the schools that portray history as it really happened. But make no mistake: the new textbooks do not talk about Saddam's glorious reign. And for the sake of the kids, we've avoided mentioning the half-million bodies we found buried in the sand, and the individual cases of abuse and torture that would horrify anyone sitting here in the Emperors Ballroom.

"I'll tell you a quick story about an Iraqi policeman whose eight-year-old son was executed," he says. "He was joking with a buddy of his in school one day and said he could run the country better than Saddam. These were the days of Saddam's secret police. The next day a group of them came into the school, grabbed the kid, took him out into the courtyard, and shot him in the head. His eight-year-old son, killed for treason."

The Emperors Ballroom gasps.

"This is the kind of evil we've encountered across the board," he says. "But we're going to fix that."

Lumer leans heavily against the podium and pushes back his glasses. "I'll tell you, we in this room are doing God's work—for a noble cause, helping these people who have suffered, and I'm proud to be here."

There's a roar of applause, and afterward a microphone is placed in the back of the room for questions.

An Iraqi man steps up to the microphone, states his name, and says he represents many Iraqi firms in Baghdad. How much hard cash, he wonders, are Iraqi firms actually getting from having 77 percent of the contracts?

Lumer says he doesn't have an exact figure, but it is "tens and tens of millions."

"Hmm," says the Iraqi man. "So out of the billions and billions, it's really only a trickle."

Lumer is exasperated. "Yes, it's only a trickle," he says. "But remember, if an Iraqi businessman makes $15 a day, he thinks he's rich."

* * *

Outside in the Emperors Foyer, cute and perky Army girls in matching shorts and T-shirts make sure everyone is on the up-

and-up. They hand out name tags, along with handsome information packets with a set of crosshairs on the cover. During a
break, the foyer fills with people looking to meet and greet. Two
camps quickly establish themselves—the eager tenderfoots
hoping to land a lucrative contract, and those already working in
Iraq and looking for more. The latter are cagey, grizzled men
with deep suntans and a tomcat look in their eyes. They stand
by the wall of windows, lighting one cigarette off another, gazing down onto the Garden of the Gods pool, where bikini girls
are already out catching the morning Nevada sun.

The foyer is the green room for the casting call, where any
supporting role in the Great Project can establish a person's
career for life. It's where Judy Ritter from New Jersey hopes to
pitch her engineering consulting firm, where Christine Bierman
from St. Louis looks to sell her line of chemical suits and gas
masks. One man owns a small airplane and wants to fly people
in and out of hot spots; there are men who sell mobile dental
vans, medical-waste incinerators, waterless showers for soldiers,
and a broad range of plastic trash bins. They're guys like Frank
Besson, a Vietnam vet who came all the way from Middleburg,
Virginia, to sell his wondrous GreenMachine, a portable inven-
tion that takes common dirt and makes bricks capable of with-
standing shrapnel and AK-47 fire.

And when the break is over, the hopeful recruits file back
into the Emperors Ballroom, and the government sends up a
battery of disciples to preach how the free market will drive
democracy in Iraq, and how the private sector must lead the way.
A tall woman in a sharp business suit from the Army Corps of
Engineers talks about "being on the front lines of freedom,"

comparing the Great Project in Iraq to our own Reconstruction after the bloody Civil War. She then invokes the words of Abraham Lincoln: "With malice toward none, with charity for all; with firmness in the right, as God gives us to see the right, let us strive on to finish the work we are in …"

The man from the Commerce Department is up next. He has a boyish grin, good hair, and looks like a Chippendale dancer. He comes in strong with the stump speech of the conference, the rallying cry of the New Gold Rush. Uncle Sam is standing like a giant Moses on the mountaintop, and this is what he sees. The vision speech is repeated in every conference in every city.

Iraq is not a poor country but a country made poor by decades of tyranny, mismanagement, and evil. Iraq has the second-largest oil reserves in the world, the largest abundance of water in the region, and enough fertile, farmable land to one day become the breadbasket of the Middle East. But we are only talking about what's belowground. Above ground there are 25 million passionate and talented people who are ready to embrace the American Dream. They are desperate to learn our way of business, eager to roll up their sleeves and work for the first time in their lives.

But more than anything, the Iraqi people want to buy things. Iraqis are demanding everything from satellite dishes and cell phones to soccer balls and tub grinders. Iraq is by far the largest emerging market of our time, and American businesses must meet the challenge. If it sells in Beaumont, it will sell in Basra. So don't languish. Decide you are not going to miss this investment opportunity of a lifetime. Decide your challenge will not be whether you go but when and how you go. When our great objective is achieved in Iraq, you will be able to say you were in on the ground floor, that you were part of the winning team.

Out of the 300 people attending the Las Vegas conference, only about half wish to actually travel to Iraq and do business. The rest are looking to sell their products or services to primes, or to Iraqi firms, from the comfort and safety of home. Whatever their plan, security plays a major role in its success, and many question if the government is painting a realistic picture of the dangers. The Vegas conference takes place three weeks after civilian contractor Nicholas Berg was kidnapped and beheaded on film by his Iraqi captors. The men and women in the Emperors Ballroom cannot help but see themselves in those images, and to help alleviate their fears the government has sent in Brigadier General Tony Hunter-Choat.

Hunter-Choat was head of security for the Coalition Provisional Authority, a retired officer in the British Special Forces who ran security for His Highness the Aga Khan and the Sultan of Oman. He is a buttoned-up Brit who stands straight as a fence and whose mouth hardly moves when speaking. He spares everyone the rosy picture and immediately cuts to the bone.

"First thing to tell you about Iraq is that it's dangerous," says Hunter-Choat. "Having said that, Iraq is a country with a superb future. The people are charming, entrepreneurial, very industrious, helpful, and kind. Of course I'm excluding those who are shooting at you and bombing you."

The General reminds everyone that the insurgents committing crimes against Americans in Iraq are a small minority. These people are rejectionists. They're rejecting democracy, capitalism, freedom of choice, and peace and prosperity for the Iraqi people.

Before you travel to Iraq, you need to know where these rejectionist elements are. You need to be prudent and have an exit strategy like in any other country. Do not check your common sense at the border. As long as you are prudent and sensible, you will make it home. There are 20,000 American contractors doing good work in Iraq, but the only ones who make the evening news are the ones who die. People die all the time. Danger is relative. Would you walk alone in Detroit at night wearing a gold watch? Of course not. Iraq is no different. If the evening news aired the grisly footage of every car accident in your town, do you think you'd still want to drive? The answer is no.

Hunter-Choat said the civilian contractors who are being targeted are those working closely with Coalition soldiers and Iraqi police. If you work outside those parameters, simple prudence will keep you safe. Men who get themselves kidnapped and killed are men who ignore procedure and operate outside the lines. They became too comfortable, and grow soft and careless. Men like Nick Berg simply strayed from the program.

"There has been no identifiable, specific threat against Western expatriate contractors," said Hunter-Choat. "And there is no indication there is going to be."

Heed the message: if you're in Iraq and find yourself being

bombed or shot at, look around—it could be a result of the
company you keep. Or worse, you have strayed from the
program.

The best way to become a sub-contractor in Iraq is to apply
online at the website of a prime who has recently been granted
a major contract. On the website, the applicant will be asked to
describe his business and how he could help the prime with a
particular project. He must be prepared to provide every detail
of his past experience, earnings, and financial standing and give
a host of references. The applicant could wait months and then
one day receive a notice indicating a particular job the prime
needs filled—for instance, that three hospitals need to be built
in Tikrit. A bidding process ensues.

Only the best of the best will survive this process, which is
what America is all about after all. If the prime doesn't weed out
the applicant, chances are the government will. Before a company gets a contract, its employees must have Defense Base Act
insurance. This is mandatory for anyone doing business over-
seas with Uncle Sam, and required before stepping foot into
Iraq. DBA insurance is your worker's compensation; it deducts
20 percent of your contract salary.

We also learn that not every prime will cover security costs,
which can deduct another 20 percent of your salary. And since
we're doing business in the Cradle of Civilization, any sub who
hits a bag of bones while digging in the desert must immediately cease all work and organize a full-scale archaeological dig,
complete with the hiring of scientists and round-the-clock security. This could last months. Contracts must be read very care-

fully. Chances are the sub will be stuck paying for this little addition to history. Finally, the government stresses that applicants be very familiar with the Federal Acquisition Regulation, which sets out the rules governing the allocation of government contract funds. Throughout the process, FAR snags will arise, and a sub must know its place within the laws. The FAR has fifty-three sections that total over 2,000 pages.

* * *

During lunch break I sit in the casino food court with Ernie Robbins, a project manager for Parsons Corporation, based in Pasadena, California. I want to know what it takes to land a contract with a prime and, with all the hurdles and mounds of red tape, if any of these men and women even stand a chance.

Robbins is impeccably dressed in a gray suit and sparkling cuff links, and he smells like expensive aftershave. He's a retired major general and a chief engineer in the Air Force, and now manages seven projects in Iraq totaling $2 billion—everything from repairing water systems to helping dispose of captured explosives. For major construction projects, he says, a prime mainly looks for companies that have worked with the government, or with a prime on an earlier project, and have a sterling reputation. A sub must come to the table with the full package. Primes do not buy commodities, they buy finished products. Companies that sell pipe will not be chosen as subs on the big projects, but those who sell pipelines will. A sub must also be ready to jump at a moment's notice, which is why it helps to have expendable capital, and lots of it, to mobilize a team and get materials in place. A sub must be ready to fork over serious cash and not expect to see black for many months.

Robbins explains how the government requires primes to spend 10 to 23 percent of their contract salary on subcontracting to small businesses. But he's not out to mislead anyone. Getting a contract is tough if you've never worked with the government or a prime, and many of these small-business owners may quickly find themselves out of the game. But the money is only beginning to flow, he says, and companies that partner with smaller firms—best of all, Iraqi firms—stand a chance of maybe a second-tier subcontract. Patience is Everything, and those who have the perseverance will still be standing when the team finally goes in for the Big Win.

"There are a lot of good deeds to be done," Robbins says. "Bringing water and electricity to these people, why in the world would they not want this? We're not there to settle the country. When we finish, nobody's going to stake out their lower forty, build fences around it, and throw a cattle farm there. We don't want a homestead. We just wanna get the work done."

In the Emperors Foyer one of the Army girls explains to an old man how to find the Romans II–IV conference rooms, where a reception is planned for the afternoon. The Army girls had been giving directions all day to people who'd gotten lost in the casino's electric maze, where signs pointing to exits and conference rooms only seemed to lead to more slot machines. The Army issued maps of the casino at registration, but most people forgot them in their rooms. The old man is from Carlsbad, California, and speaks with a German accent. He tells the girls he hasn't been able to find his room since breakfast. He doubts he will ever find Romans II–IV.

"Well, here's how I remember," says the Army girl. "When you come to that eighteen-foot statue of Caesar, just turn left. Now how hard is that?"

Always be partnering. Partnering with Iraqis not only pro-
vides Americans with associates who possess market knowl-
edge and generations of contacts; it also allows Iraqis to
feel like they're taking part in their own reconstruction.

The reception in Romans II–IV provides an exceptional partnering opportunity. The two dozen Iraqis attending the conference can finally meet their American counterparts and discuss teaming up in the desert. Since Americans aren't allowed to buy property in Iraq, only lease, Iraqis can scout out empty warehouses or abandoned factories, and help smooth the transaction. To the Iraqis, the Americans can provide commodities that Iraqis have been desperate for during their long period of sleep. Amid the low rumble of voices, you can hear Frank Besson, loaded with a stack of Green-Machine pamphlets, cornering an Iraqi man, telling him, "They're called TerraBricks, and these suckers will last 2,000 years …" Afterward, the Iraqis break off into their own groups, debating in Arabic and sending the waiters back to refill the vegetable tray.

Among the two dozen Iraqis in the room are Subhi and Mohammed Khudairi, who've come to Vegas with their father, Aziz. They're looking for potential investors to help salvage their family's paint and beverage factories in Baghdad, which crumbled during sanctions. Worse, the paint factory was recently shelled by American forces.

The Khudairis belong to one of the oldest merchant families in Iraq, a lineage that dates back hundreds of years. Twenty years ago, Aziz brought the family to Houston and has shuttled back and forth to Baghdad ever since. Mohammed and Subhi both graduated from the University of Texas at Austin, were esteemed members of the rowdy Kappa Alpha fraternity, and Mohammed ran in the same circles as Jenna Bush, the President's daughter.

In Romans II–IV, the Khudairi sons are dressed in sharp, designer suits and look like J. Crew models; both admit that their Arabic rings with a Texas twang. Whereas Mohammed's dark hair and complexion peg him as Arab, Subhi is fair-skinned, and his wavy hair is golden blond. Subhi recently quit his job as an equities trader at AIM Investments and now looks to "modernize" the family dynasty before it's rendered obsolete in the rush of American corporations. His girlfriend is blonde and pretty, the way a cheer-leader is pretty, and has made it clear she doesn't want him going to Iraq. But after he took one of his buddies to Amman one summer, there's now a line of frat boys looking to hit the war zone with their own personal guide. "My friends," he says, "used to call me the Wacky Iraqi."

* * *

The primes stand along the wall in front of foldaway display booths that are stacked with glossy literature and adorned with enlarged photos of men wearing hard hats in the desert. A line quickly forms at each booth. For the American small business-men and –women, the reception is the conference's main event, possibly the only opportunity to have any face time with the big boys. Many take a moment to work up their nerve by hitting the cash bar or find comfort in the fried-burrito buffet. Clouds of cigarette smoke waft in from the hallway. Everyone knows that once he reaches the head of the line, there's only five minutes to make his pitch.

Yes, be sure to study your FARs and know your DBAs, and take pride in knowing that you're the best damn plumbing-supply man in southern Illinois. But if you're given five minutes and you choke, if you enter the golden window and fall to pieces, chances are you will not be cast in this great ballet in the desert. Your business card will be lost and your phone will not ring. It's this dogfight spirit that makes America great, where only the strong and hungry of heart claw their way to the top, while the weak and ill-prepared are burned as fuel to keep the Vegas Strip blazing through the night.

Dale and Jan Durham work the room like assassins, finishing with one prime, then jumping to the line of another. Under one arm, Dale holds a leather briefcase the size of a hatbox. His gray suit is outdated, but he wears it well. He has a thin face, a beard, and brown wispy hair. When he speaks to a prime, his body language is relaxed and puts the men at ease. But Dale is not at ease. Dale and Jan have come all the way from Shreveport, Louisiana, holding their guts in their hands.

Dale and Jan own an engineer-support business, designing and drafting blueprints of finished buildings. This is all done by computer, and since everything in Iraq has been done by hand, Dale is confident the primes could use his service.

Five years ago, Dale had fifteen employees and was pulling down nearly half a million a year in business. He bought some land and built a house and took out a loan from the bank. Just about then the economy crumbled. Companies stopped building in Shreveport. Now Dale has only two employees and goes a month or two without a job. The mortgage on the house is eating him alive. Somehow the house became collateral on the business and the business became collateral on the house. And to top it off, he's got two kids waiting to go to college.

So when Dale saw on CNN that Congress had approved that $18.4 billion, he told Jan he wanted to go to Iraq.

Dale is a former soldier, a First Armored Division tank commander and certified "top gun." He served most of his time in Germany during the 1970s, where he learned to hit a coffee can with a 105mm tank shell at 2,000 meters.

Dale says he is not afraid of Iraq, but it wasn't the Army that made him hard. Dale grew up in a tiny sawmill town in East Texas, poor and fatherless. His mother raised him on her paltry wages from a furniture factory, and her brothers and nephews made sure he learned to fight, usually by just beating his ass. He prowled the honky-tonks and became "a damn good instigator" and all around hell-raiser. The military taught him discipline, but it was Jan who came along and straightened him out, made him want to be a better man. "She made me finally feel safe in my life," says Dale.

Dale says he was aware of the dangers, about Nick Berg and Thomas Hamill and snipers perched in the underpasses. He knows that a dead husband provides nothing but grief. But in his core, Iraq is calling him.

"He's like a little boy sometimes," says Jan. "He actually wants to be there."

Dale says, "I grew up in an atmosphere where I'm most comfortable in conflict." Jan just shakes her head.

True to his profession, Dale has designed mental storyboards and blue-prints for every possible scenario he might face if given a contract. And there are requirements that must be met—certain things to justify the danger and loneliness in the desert. Of course, the job has to make money for both himself and the prime; that way both teams are happy. But most of all, he says, it has to be something positive for the Iraqi people, "something a proud man can be proud of."

"People are going back to school and work for the first time in years," says Jan. "For the first time, they're getting a good life, and he can be part of that."

"It's a win-win situation," says Dale.

"And look at all the debt we can pay off," says Jan. "This is a good thing for us."

Dale nods his head. "It's the only thing."

By the time the reception is over, Dale and Jan manage to pitch every prime in the room. The only solid lead comes from a man from Con-track International, who asks if Dale would be interested in training Iraqis to use the drafting software. In the middle of the conversation, the man stops and looks Dale in the eyes. "Tell me straight," the man says. "Are you *really* willing to go to Iraq?" Dale never hesitates.

Afterward we go for a drink at the Galleria Bar, where a lounge act plays quietly in the corner. The bar is open to the casino floor, where old women in tank tops sit catatonic in front of the flashing wheels. Dale orders a coffee and says he wants to show me something. He unzips his leather briefcase and holds it open. Inside are files three inches thick on every prime that had stood in Romans II–IV, complete with company histories, earning reports, and contracting preferences.

"I could tell you what those guys eat for breakfast," says Dale. "And you talk about the FAR. I've read every damn page."

"As you can tell," says Jan, "we've been waiting for this conference for months."

Dale teases Jan about being a "city girl" who's hardly ever left Shreve-port, and tells a funny story about the time she tried cleaning catfish. Jan teases Dale about wearing his "city shoes" for the first time in years—a pair of black tasseled loafers— instead of his everyday cowboy boots. It's Dale's first time in Vegas, but there will be no gambling. Most of their savings went toward plane tickets and three nights at Caesars Palace.

"It's appropriate they had this conference in a casino," says Dale, staring into the sea of lights and machines. He shakes a pair of imaginary dice in his fist, blows on them for luck, and sends them tumbling across the table. "Here's to everything," he says.

* * *

That night I leave my room and wander through the casino. It's late, and Caesars Palace buzzes with those still chasing the edge of a dream, diehards who take their nourishment from cocktails of bottled oxygen and watered-down gin, and who never question time.

A shirtless man dressed as Caesar and carrying a sword passes me near the registration desk. His muscles glisten under the lights, and gold leaves shimmer in his hair. Two buxom women in bikini tops hug each arm while the three of them pose for photos with a group of plump schoolteachers. There's the fraternity man with a bull neck and apple cheeks, who lips a cigar as he drags his drunk sobbing girlfriend behind him; the lone Chinese man who stands at the baccarat table, staring down the dealer with a look that could cut a diamond; teenage girls in see-through skirts smoking cigarettes and gazing through expensive shop windows. Everywhere I turn there are honeymooners.

I find a seat at the Shadow Bar and order a beer. Two girls dance topless behind a silk screen, their lithe arms and fingers snaking above their faceless heads like black smoke. Like Vegas, Iraq can be anything to everyone: a magic portal out of hard times, or a sparkling mirage that evaporates with you inside. It has become Dale's golden key, and with him still fresh in my mind, I'm reminded of another man I met a few weeks before.

I ran into Gerald Flannery in Lansing, Michigan, at a similar conference on doing business in Iraq. He'd hobbled into the conference room using a walking stick decorated with Indian beads and crystals. His silver hair was long in back, but his beard was neatly trimmed. He'd struck up a conversation with one of the government officials, something about the war and all the negative news and how Michigan could use some contracts in Iraq. "Yep," said Gerald, heading toward his chair. "As soon as I get my back fixed, I'm gonna strap on an AK-47 and see what I can do over there."

I immediately introduced myself and made arrangements to meet later that afternoon. When he handed me his business card, I noticed a tattoo of a pentagram on the back of his hand.

Gerald's house was south of Flint, a hulking tri-level home on five acres surrounded by thick forest. When I pulled into the drive, he was out in the yard.

"Saw a wounded hawk when I pulled up a while ago," said Gerald, pointing into the trees. "Damn dogs must've scared him off."

We stood there a couple of minutes looking for the wounded hawk, but finally gave up and went inside.

Gerald's wife was out for the afternoon, so the two of us sat around the bar in the kitchen. Gerald poured himself a glass of red wine, and for the next two hours he explained how an opportunity like Iraq could be an answer for almost everything wrong in his world—from the encroachment of "Red China" on Michigan's working people to his own engulfing darkness.

The way Gerald saw it, outsourcing to China was gutting Michigan's once-booming industry of auto-parts manufacturers. Men who once pulled down six-figure salaries were now filling out applications at Wal-Mart. Eight million of the nation's manufacturing jobs have vanished since 1990. Gerald hadn't escaped the damage: after twenty years in business, he was forced to merge his gauge-manufacturing company with a big firm, which eventually squeezed him out.

As president of the Michigan Tooling Association, which represents 750 statewide tool-and-die companies, Gerald sees Iraq as a way for his guys to get back on their feet and save their companies from the auction block. Of course, they face the same hurdles and red tape as everyone else: the challenge of finding Iraqi business partners, guys you could trust to arrange things on that end. And no one really knows how damaged the manufacturing infrastructure is, especially after all the bombing. What small businessman can afford to build a factory in a war zone?

Gerald said he couldn't personally go at least until his back was better. Years of martial arts eventually wore away two lower vertebrae, which will require major surgery. His health in general, he said, was not very good.

"There's also my wife," Gerald said. His mood darkened considerably. "She promised an instant divorce if I went to Iraq."

Three years ago, Gerald's son was killed when the four-wheeler he'd been driving slammed into a tree. He was twenty years old. Gone, just like that. The boy riding with him walked away with barely a scratch. Gerald's son was his best friend; he'd taught the kid everything, and they were hardly ever apart. And when he died, so did Gerald's will to live. After the funeral, he told his wife he was only sticking around for their twenty-seven-year-old daughter.

"What do I have to lose?" he said. "Not a lot. Every day of my life is hell. It's like a goddamn movie that never stops."

Gerald explained how Iraq was his Big Out. It had nothing to do with making money or paying bills. It was just a way to end a sick, tormented life without having to do the messy work himself. Gerald wanted to die like a man, and with a bang if he could.

"I'd just as soon jump in a cargo plane full of Rangers and shoot till I'm dead," he said. He rubbed his beard and smiled.

The words coming out of his mouth seemed to surprise him. "I'd much rather die by the sword than sitting in a chair."

Talking about his son seemed to open a dark spillway in Gerald's soul, or maybe it was just the wine. He then told me he kept closets full of guns and assault rifles. He had studied various religions and the occult as a young man, which explained the pentagram tattoo. He was part Crow, part Blackfoot, and had two large tribal tattoos on both of his meaty shoulders. The concept of tribalism had fascinated him throughout his life, and this knowledge helped him understand the Middle East. Terrorism in Iraq and Israel can be defeated by thinking in tribalistic terms, he said. For instance, send an army into Fallujah and Gaza and start systematically killing people, even women and kids, until the mullahs realize you mean business.

"Once their seed is threatened," he said, "they'll rethink their terror tactics."

Gerald opened the door and let in his dogs, two hulking gray Bouviers that jumped into my lap, all round happy eyes and wet tongues. Their attention quickly turned to a muted television in the corner of the room. Two men on-screen were having a fist fight, and both dogs started flipping out, barking and jumping around the room.

"They don't like violence," said Gerald. "Weirdest thing."

I had a long drive ahead of me, so I thanked Gerald for his hospitality and got up to leave. Be careful out there, he said, and I told him to let me know when he finally made the big plunge. His handshake was tight, and I couldn't help but wonder if he was looking for his son as he held on. We made plans to talk again, traded email addresses, and said goodbye. When I pulled out of the drive, I saw him gaze out across the yard, looking for that wounded hawk.

*   *   *

On the last day in Vegas, there's a continental breakfast in the Emperors Foyer, followed by a lecture on true grit. Major James Blanco, from the Army's Small Business Office, reminds everyone that Iraq isn't the junior varsity. Iraq is a high-stakes blood sport played by men with balls the size of Big Wheels. Men who could morph their bodies into polished steel from pure will alone and fly there themselves. This is nothing like doing business in Canada. "Iraq is the game we're playing here, folks," he reminds us. "And if you're not willing to spend $79 a night at Caesars Palace to find out about multibillion-dollar opportunities, then you better think again about what you're doing."

Major Blanco then teaches us how to navigate the Small Business Office's website, which he designed himself. The website appears on a giant screen, and Major Blanco tells us to pay close attention. We start with a virtual tour of the office, which begins with a helicopter landing on an airstrip outside the Pentagon and a super soldier named Sergeant Hoo-ah leading the group through the warrens of the building. At one point, Sergeant Hoo-ah takes us through a door where images of combat soldiers splash across the screen, from grunts in wigs fighting the Revolutionary War to the hard-bitten Rangers storming the desert in Iraq.

"This is my own personal tribute," says Major Blanco, gazing up at the screen. "I'm still moved every time I see it."

Major Blanco tells us he'd been depressed about missing the war and not getting any trigger time, knowing his buddies would return as Minotaurs while he pushed paper for the Man. But after attending these conferences, and later hearing the stories of success and fortune, he soon realized the battlefield wasn't where victory would be won. Iraq will be won by the men and women in this room, the rank and file of Main Street, because commerce is our greatest weapon against terror and evil. Major Blanco stands tall, a born-again hacker, and tells us, "I realized then I had the greatest job of my life."

Afterward, Mark Lumer returns to the stage to tell us another story about how the American way is conquering darkness: An Iraqi contractor walks into the Coalition headquarters one day to get paid for a project he'd just completed. The roll desk says, "Absolutely, sir. Come this way." There are no banks in Iraq, so the American takes the Iraqi down into the vault, where there's millions of dollars in cash. He counts out $25,000 and places the stack in front of the Iraqi contractor. "Thank you for your hard work, sir," says the American payroll man. "Now just sign here." The Iraqi signs his name to the ledger, but then he just stands there. The American tells him, "There's your money, you're free to go." The Iraqi replies, "I understand," but still he stands there. The American says, "Really, sir, you can take your money." "I understand," says the Iraqi, but he doesn't move. Finally, the American says, "Well, what in hell are you waiting for?" The Iraqi says, "For you to take your cut." The American payroll man looks the Iraqi dead in the eyes and tells him, "Sir, that is not the way we do business in America." Streams of tears begin to roll down the Iraqi contractor's face. Overcome with emotion, he grabs the American payroll man and kisses him on both cheeks.

*   *   *

The Emperors Ballroom explodes with whooping and applause, a swell of patriotism and pride so fierce it nearly lifts the Palace Tower off its foundation. The pent-up emotion is overwhelming, and I myself am overwhelmed with an ecstatic vision of the tower rising up from the Vegas Strip and into the clear blue afternoon sky. With Lumer steering our course from the podium, we kiss the stratosphere and rocket through at the awesome speed of light. Within minutes, Earth appears on the giant screen. Then, as we get closer, we see a brilliant glow, so bright it hurts to look.

"The future!" shouts Lumer.

It's a golden city, sparkling in the desert sun. The Tigris and Euphrates glisten like a string of jewels. There are no sounds of gunfire, only the evanescence of children singing. As we hover closer, we can see the great fruits of our victory: every street is gloriously choked with traffic, and there's a satellite dish perched atop every roof. We hold one another and cry tears of joy.

*   *   *

By the end of the afternoon, I manage to escape the Emperors Ballroom and head toward the casino floor. As I cruise down the escalator, I realize I haven't been outside in three days. I dash through the catacomb of lights, past cigarette girls and crowds of the walking dead, until I'm outside under an open sky, breathing the fresh sultry Vegas air. It's near twilight, and a three-quarter moon hangs above the Strip just like another tourist attraction.

Dale was right: it was fitting that they'd held this conference at a casino. He'd implied the gamble, of course, but the real message goes well beyond that. *Here was democracy on the head of a pin, everything worth defending and carrying on our backs to those less fortunate. It glittered and beeped and danced naked behind the bar. It instantly made you rich, or slowly bled you clean. But at least it allowed you to try. It was freedom, as pure as the oxygen pumped through the vents. And it is why they hate us, those rejectionists with their primitive ways and the goddamn chip on their shoulders. They hate us because we're happy.*

I reach the Bellagio Hotel just in time for the famous light show. Every twenty minutes 1,000 fountains in front of the palatial hotel do their own water dance with beams of light and music. I join the crowd of people along the fountain rail, many of them tourists from other countries dressed in shorts and sun visors. We check our watches and jostle for space, not wanting to miss a second. The show begins with spectacular pomp: all at once the music trumpets from a perimeter of speakers as the fountain comes alive in shoots of water and colored light. The music is none other than Lee Greenwood singing "God Bless the USA," and I search the fountain rail for Mark Lumer or Major Blanco, winking as they harness the daydream. Instead I see several men removing their hats, staring wide-eyed into the pulsing light. I want to climb the rail and shout, "This is not our anthem!" But the song reaches its crashing finale, and we all crane our heads toward the sky. The water bursting into the air sounds exactly like cannons.

Bryan Mealer writes for *Harper's Magazine*.

A Puppet for All Seasons

Susan Watkins

'His Majesty's Government and I are in the same boat and must sink or swim together ... if you wish me and your policy to succeed, it is folly to damn me permanently in the public eye by making me an obvious puppet.'

King Faisal I to the British high commissioner, Mesopotamia,
August 17, 1921

Rarely has a passage of powers been so furtive. The ceremony on June 28—held two days ahead of schedule, deep within Baghdad's fortified Green Zone—lasted just ten minutes, with thirty U.S. and Iraqi officials present. Outside the concrete stockade, the military realities have remained the same: an occupation force of 160,000 U.S.-led troops, an additional army of commercial security guards, and jumpy ill-equipped local police units. Before departing, the Coalition Provisional Authority set in place a parallel government structure of commissioners and inspectors general who, elections notwithstanding, will control

Iraq's chief ministries for the next five years. The largest U.S. embassy in the world will dominate Baghdad, with regional "hubs" planned in Mosul, Kirkuk, Hilla, and Basra. Most of the billions in reconstruction money that has been contracted so far is being spent on American military bases. The U.N. has resolved that the country's oil revenues will continue to be deposited in the U.S.-dominated Development Fund, again for the next five years. The Allawi government will have no authority to reallocate contracts signed by the CPA, largely with foreign companies that remain above the law of the land. A majority of current Iraqi cabinet ministers are themselves U.S. or U.K. citizens.

Iyad Allawi, hailed in the Western media as the blunt, independent-minded leader the country needs, is an appropriate appointment as prime minister. Little secret is made of the fact that, like his counterpart Hamid Karzai in Afghanistan, he has been a paid CIA agent for many years; such a record is no longer considered something to hide. Allawi's career to date has more than qualified him for his present role. Iraqis recall him as a Baath enforcer in London student circles of the 1970s, with a bogus medical degree conferred by the regime for services rendered. According to his former colleague Dirgam Kadhim, Allawi was simultaneously dealing with MI6 (a branch of the British intelligence services) and running a Mukhabarat death squad for Saddam's faction of the Baath, targeting dissenters in Europe—until falling foul of the party himself by the late '70s. After a few years in hiding he resurfaced in Amman, co-founding the Iraqi National Accord with Salih Omar Ali al-Tikriti, said to be a former supervisor of public hangings in Baghdad. The

INA specialized in recruiting military and intelligence defectors; the bomb blasts attributed to it in the mid-90s—one in a crowded theater, another killing schoolchildren on a bus—were purportedly "proficiency tests" set by the CIA. Duly persuaded of the INA's merits, the agency provided funding for Allawi's botched coup attempt of 1996 that, uncovered by Saddam, resulted in more than a hundred executions. He was subsequently responsible for passing on the intelligence that prompted Tony Blair's claim of forty-five-minute WMD delivery systems, and pinpointed Saddam's supposed bunker for bombardment at the start of the invasion.

With the U.S. occupation established, Allawi was put on the Governing Council in charge of security. His campaign for the post of prime minister—his lobbying firm spent over $340,000—was naturally run in Washington, not Baghdad. Once appointed, he embarrassed his masters by threatening to proclaim martial law before his inauguration. His colleague Ghazi al-Yawar, Iraq's new president, made a comparable show of independence by demurring from Bush's proposal to blow up Abu Ghraib: it would be a pity to demolish the prison when the Americans had spent so much money on it. Yawar, who was running an obscure telecoms firm in Saudi Arabia when the United States established contact with him before the invasion, began dressing up in Shammar tribal robes as soon as he was put on the Governing Council, perhaps on a tip from Karzai in Afghanistan.

* * *

That it took Washington more than a year to erect such a thread-
bare front—Karzai was parachuted into place within a matter of
weeks—is testimony to the strength of the Iraqi resistance. How
should such a force be gauged? In June 1940 the French Army,
like its modern Iraqi counterpart, collapsed in the face of the
German *Blitzkrieg* without a serious fight, and within a month
French National Assembly deputies gathered at Vichy had voted,
569–80, in favor of a collaborationist regime under Marshal
Pétain. The Vichy government was swiftly recognized by the
United States and other powers, and the majority of non-Jewish
French settled down to life under the occupation. It was two
years before the maquis began to offer serious resistance.
Elsewhere in Europe, the pattern was similar. The Germans were
efficient in organizing indigenous support: Quisling in Norway,
the Croatian Ustashi and SS-trained Bosnian and Kosovar regi-
ments in Yugoslavia, the Iron Guard in Romania, the Arrow
Cross in Hungary. In their classical form, twentieth-century
resistance movements were slow to constitute themselves, and
those that did appear nearly always had external state support.
The Allies' supplies were crucial to the anti-Nazi underground
of Continental Europe, and the general pattern was much the
same in Asia and Africa. Chinese weaponry was a condition of
Vietminh victory, as Egyptian and Tunisian backing was for the
FLN in Algeria. Typically, such foreign help functioned in con-
junction with an already existing political leadership and party
network with a potential for hegemony at a national level, as with
the local Communist movements in France, Italy, or Indochina.

The resistance that has emerged over the past eighteen
months to the U.S. occupation in Iraq fits none of these cate-

gories. It began early, the first armed attacks erupting in May 2003, within weeks of Baghdad's fall. It escalated over the summer, as demonstrations and street protests were regularly fired upon. The initial hit-and-miss harrying of the occupation force had developed by August 2003 into assaults on strategic military and diplomatic targets such as the Jordanian embassy and the U.N. compound. By November of that year, U.S. forces were suffering heavier losses, with the insurgents bringing down helicopters. Vicious reprisals led to a further escalating spiral. Like any other military occupation, the Anglo-American regime has been one of sanctioned murder and torture, and the resistance to it has been similarly savage. Suicide raids, car bombs, and mortars have sown havoc in the big cities, taking a terrible toll. By mid-October, U.S. forces were contending with an average of sixty-five attacks every day. Increasingly sophisticated assaults on pipelines and pumping stations (more than 2,000 in the past year) have cut oil exports for weeks at a time. What triggered most alarm for Western and Arab governments, however, was the simultaneous rebellion that broke out across the Shia south and Sunni centre in April 2004, the joint Shia–Sunni convoy from Baghdad to Fallujah, and other prefigurations of a national resistance leadership—Washington's great fear. Meanwhile, the occupation's own polls measured the solid bank of popular support behind the fighters.

Externally, the Iraqi resistance faces a front of unprecedented official hostility—a global unanimity unimaginable in any previous age. U.N. Security Council Resolution 1546, passed in June, extends unqualified support to the U.S.-appointed Allawi regime, conferring the full legitimacy of the "international community" on its collection of old CIA hands and carpetbaggers. Explaining that the country—lacking an army, and with a transparent absence of WMDs—"continues to constitute a threat to international peace and security," it authorizes the occupying force to take "all necessary measures"; i.e., whatever American commanders deem fit. All U.N. members are, of course, bluntly prohibited from supplying arms or materiel to the Iraqi people. France and Germany offered the comedy of a request that sovereign control over the occupier's army be entrusted to the Iraqi façade it has manufactured—only to be told by Allawi's foreign minister that Paris and Berlin should not be "more Iraqi than the Iraqis," who desired only that the U.S. command "keep them informed."

Politically, the Iraqi resistance has been heterogeneous and fragmentary, lacking the established party networks crucial to most previous anti-occupation movements. It includes former Baathists, secular liberals and social democrats, multi-hued mosque-based networks, and splits from the collaborationist Iraqi Communist and Dawa parties; the most authoritative reports suggest surprisingly low figures for international jihadist involvement. Ideologically, nationalism and Islamism—"for God and Iraq"—are the most potent calls, but there are elements of Third World anti-imperialism and pan-Arabism too. It remains to be seen whether these groups can establish some equivalent of a national liberation front, to unite religious and secular groups around the central demand for the expulsion of all foreign troops.

Externally isolated and internally unsynchronized, the Iraqi maquis nevertheless possesses a number of distinct resources.

First, strong social networks: resilient clan and extended-family connections; cohesive neighbourhood quarters; and mosques that offer a local sanctuary and gathering place, unimaginable in occupied Europe. Arab writers have pointed out the attendant weaknesses of these forms: particularism, local rivalry, lack of coordination, the treachery or opportunism of unaccountable demagogues, a fringe of criminality thriving on the social breakdown. Yet within this fluid, vocal, and highly mobilized environment, leaders can be forced into taking more resolute stands to retain the loyalty of their supporters.

Second, unlike previous anti-occupation movements, the Iraqi resistance has at its disposal sufficient explosives to harry the occupiers for years to come, in the dumps of conventional weaponry (rocket launchers, artillery shells, etc.) accrued by the previous regime. Shock-resistant, these weapons have to be painstakingly dismantled, one by one; an attempt to blow up an ammunition stack simply scatters it, unexploded. The United States has only a few hundred engineers in Iraq capable of the task.

Third, the natural dislike of any people for a foreign occupation has been reinforced by the stark deterioration of social conditions since the Anglo-American invasion. In much of the countryside, the long-term agrarian crisis—salination, pump failure, silted canals—has worsened as agribusiness imports increase. Rising rural unemployment has swelled the slum populations of Basra and Baghdad. Much of Iraq's industrial sector—already skewed toward arms production during the Iran-Iraq war, then targeted by Western bombs in the 1990s—faces not privatization but closure, putting a skilled workforce on the street. Indeed, two thirds of the pre-invasion labor force may now be unemployed. A deepening social crisis is concealed behind the daily military communiques, and the occupation presence provides a tangible target for Iraqis' frustrations.

Finally, the resistance can draw upon vivid historical memories of triumphant battles against the last imperial occupier. The modern Iraqi nation is a creation of the struggle against British colonialism, after London seized Mesopotamia from Istanbul in 1917. The countrywide uprising in the summer of 1920 forced Britain to retreat from direct administration on the Delhi model, and its solution—"ruling without governing," or "exercising control through an ostensibly independent native government"—was to set up a monarchy dependent on British arms for survival and backed by a League of Nations mandate authorizing all necessary measures. The British high commissioner remained the highest power in the land, and, when the mandate expired, the Anglo-Iraqi Treaty guaranteed British control over Iraq's foreign policy, seaport, railways, airbases, and, in times of war, security forces. Compliant local notables signed on to the treaty, but the majority of the population rejected it. When resistance broke out in 1922, the British high commissioner arrested political leaders, banned nationalist parties, and famously subdued rebellious tribes with punitive bombing and mustard gas.

But despite London's efforts to foster conservative landlordism in the countryside, packing tame national assemblies with loyal sheikhs, urban social forces could not be held down indefinitely. In April 1941 the pro-British regent, the crown prince, and the prime minister were forced to flee abroad when pan-Arab officers with mass nationalist backing seized power and abrogated the wartime provisos of the treaty. The U.K. had to reoccupy the country to restore imperial control, returning the crown prince to Baghdad in a British tank. In January 1948 popular anger at the recycling of the treaty and at the British role in Palestine set off an insurrectionary movement in the capital, mingling middle-class students and nationalists with communist railway workers and slum dwellers. Finally, after a decade of suppressed revolts, a coup toppled the monarchy with the backing of both Communists and Baathists (at that time a small party with under a thousand members). Huge crowds clogged the streets to block any counterrevolution as the Republic of Iraq was proclaimed by a left-nationalist government and the door to national independence and social reform was flung open at last.

Iraqis are well tutored in these battles, the ABCs of their modern history. But the past rarely offers exact analogies, and to view contemporary events through its lens highlights differences as well as similarities between the old imperial occupation and the new. Militarily and politically, the machinery of American power in Iraq today is far more formidable than Britain's was. With 160,000 troops at his disposal, Ambassador John Negroponte has a greater vice-regal command of violence than the British high commissioner ever possessed. American control of Iraqi harbors, airports, and security forces—not to speak of courts, education, trade, finance, media, and foreign policy—has been given the U.N. seal, with a force of "international law" going well beyond the bilateral Anglo-Iraqi treaty. Washington's coffers are deeper than London's ever were, and today's oil revenues were undreamed of in the 1920s. The capacity of the occupation to buy consent is far higher. It can also hope to rely on the sheer exhaustion and dislocation of life after March 2003 to create a longing for some semblance of normalcy, under new arrangements that promise to transfer, however nominally, elements of sovereignty back to the country.

*   *   *

It would be a mistake therefore to think that nothing has changed since L. Paul Bremer flew out and Negroponte flew in. As in the German-occupied Europe of 1940-41, native collaborationist regimes typically offer some initial degree of relief after the humiliation of foreign invasion, as well as lucrative business or administrative positions to servants of the new order. The puppet government in Baghdad today enjoys far less autonomy than Pétain's regime in Vichy—in that respect it is closer to Quisling's in Oslo—but it has a basis of support from an array of privileged groups in the post-invasion landscape— not just carpetbaggers on CIA or MI6 payrolls but technocrats eyeing career opportunities, a swath of the semi-expatriate bourgeoisie and the sanction-busting nouveaux riches, traditionally collaborationist rural families, and the large Kurdish population in the north. Crucially, the regime has also enjoyed the tolerance of the Shia hierarchy around Ayatollah al-Sistani, airlifted to London for the duration of last August's siege of Najaf.

All this, however, must contend with the Arab population's hatred for the American occupation itself. The foreign hand is everywhere visible in the new Iraq. Even in the north, where U.S.

troops are scarcely needed, the Kurdish leadership has installed a network of Israeli intelligence agents and hit squads, the culmination of its disastrous record of political misjudgments. If its client regime is not to be permanently associated with American bombers, tanks, and jails, the United States urgently needs an effective native enforcement body. Yet, despite the level of unemployment, enlistments are still lagging far below planned figures, the loyalty of new recruits remains in doubt, and Allawi's attempts to brigade or buy over former Baath officers have not yet produced any better results.

On the ideological front there is little more light. Under rules endorsed by U.N. Resolution 1546, the January 2005 election allows Iraqis to choose candidates selected by the U.S. embassy for a "transitional" administration with strictly limited powers, charged with drafting a constitution for a further, equally restricted ballot by January 2006. The hand-picked, thousand-member consultative conference convened in August proved a complete fiasco, with Allawi's thugs ejecting all critics.

Internationally, the regime and its masters look forward to strengthening their position by planting the U.N. flag once again in Iraqi soil, but so far the Secretariat has not dared to return to Baghdad, with good reason. On conservative estimates, some 300,000 children under five died from disease and malnutrition under the U.N. sanctions regime of the 1990s, while the Secretariat skimmed administration fees of over $1 billion. In 1998 the U.N. contracts committee awarded the Oil for Food Programme contract for monitoring Iraqi imports (of often rotted food and diluted medicines) to Cotecna Inspection, a company that employed Kofi Annan's son Kojo as a consultant throughout the bidding process. In June, U.N. special envoy Lakhdar Brahimi, a leading member of the junta that canceled elections in Algeria in 1992 and broker of the Karzai regime in Afghanistan, rubber-stamped Bremer's selection of members of the Governing Council for reincarnation as ministers of the Interim Government; but, duty performed, could not wait to get out. When they do return, U.N. functionaries will need a large private army of their own to protect them.

* * *

Formally speaking, the Anglo-American invasion has been stripped of its original pretexts. There were no weapons of mass destruction. Human-rights violations have branded the liberators. The need to bring democracy to Iraq, let alone the rest of the Middle East, has become less pressing. It is the strength of the Iraqi resistance—and it alone—that has led to widespread uneasiness in the Western establishments. Washington think tanks have been buzzing about exit strategies, estimating the costs to U.S. political credibility ("high, or unacceptable?"), assessing "indicators for withdrawal." The American electorate has turned against the war: a fluctuating majority of voters now think the invasion was a mistake.

Yet those who shook their heads at the pre-emptive proclamations of the 2002 National Security Strategy have been strangely unwilling to see it founder. With the upsurge of resistance in Iraq has come a flood of liberal-imperialist advice on how to run the occupation better. Joseph Nye laments the failure of American TV channels to beam U.S. soft power into the

Arab world. Anthony Cordesman offers more effective interrogation methods than those practiced at Abu Ghraib. Michael Ignatieff, after deploring the painful moral juxtapositions of torture images that sullied even Reagan's funeral, warns that America "cannot abdicate its responsibility."

From those who opposed the Anglo-American invasion in 2003 on the grounds that it lacked U.N. legitimation, or that sanctions were doing the job, there has been, understandably, a deafening silence about the future of the occupation. For many, opposition to U.S. policy in Iraq has been reduced to anathematizing Bush. But good as it would have been to see the Bush Administration punished at the polls, hopes that Kerry would do more than repackage current policies in the Middle East were futile. Bush has already implemented every step of his challenger's program (NATO, U.N., multinational conferences). Indeed, Robert Kagan suggested that a Democratic administration was the necessary next step in consolidating the 2002 National Security Strategy: "It is important for the Democrats to own the war on terrorism and not simply be the opposition. Also, we would have a fresh start with the Europeans and other allies, though they would quickly be disillusioned to learn that Kerry wouldn't be that different from Bush in some respects." In other words, the Bush revolution will have succeeded in producing its heir.

Regardless of which multimillionaire sits in the White House, the reality is that, so long as hard blows continue to be inflicted by the resistance on the occupying army and its clients, domestic support for the recolonization of Iraq will drain away. The same holds true of Europe, where Paris and Berlin have predictably hastened to patch up their relations with Washington and approved NATO engagement to support its Baghdad regime; in the case of Jacques Chirac, sealing the pact with the Franco-American invasion of Haiti and the U.N.-backed over-throw of the constitutional government there. The disagree-ments that in the spring of 2003 supposedly threatened the Atlantic alliance have been ceremoniously buried in the Normandy sands, in County Clare, and in Istanbul. Washington's military-imperialist thrust into central Eurasia, at first deplored by right-minded pillars of the status quo as an overreaching adventure, has become the basis of a new world consensus: the hegemon must not be allowed to fail. Such unanimity, however, does not alter the fact that the U.S.-led forces have no business in Iraq, or that the Iraqi people have every right to drive them out.

Susan Watkins is editor of the *New Left Review*.

No Terrorism

The Terrorism to Come

Walter Laqueur

Terrorism has become, over a number of years, a topic of ceaseless comment and controversy, and it now figures prominently on the national and international agenda. It is one of the most emotionally charged topics of public debate, though quite why this should be the case is not entirely clear, as those taking part in the debate do not sympathize with terrorism.

Confusion prevails, but confusion alone does not explain the emotions. There is always confusion when a new international phenomenon appears on the scene. This was the case, for instance, with Communism, which was thought initially to be aiming at the nationalization of women and the burning of priests.

Thirty years ago, when the terrorism debate got under way, it was widely asserted that terrorism was a left-wing revolutionary movement caused by oppression and exploitation. Hence the conclusion: find a political and social solution, remedy the underlying evil—no oppression, no terrorism. The argument about the left-wing character of terrorism is no longer frequently heard, but the belief in a fatal link between poverty and violence has persisted. Whenever a major terrorist attack occurs, one hears appeals from high and low to provide credits and loans, to deal at long last with the deeper, true causes of terrorism, the roots rather than the outward manifestations. And these roots are believed to be poverty, unemployment, and inequality.

It is not too difficult to debunk the correlation between poverty and terrorism; indeed, the experts have long maintained that poverty does not cause terrorism and prosperity does not cure it. Terrorists are not poor people and do not come from poor societies. In the world's fifty poorest countries, there is little or no terrorism. A recent study of India noted that terrorism there has occurred in the most prosperous (Punjab) and most egalitarian (Kashmir) regions and that, on the other hand, the poorest regions such as North Bihar have been free of terrorism. In Arab countries, the terrorists hail not from the poorest and most neglected districts but from places with concentrations of radical preachers. The backwardness, if any, is intellectual and cultural, not economic and social.

These findings, however, have had little impact on public opinion (or on politicians), and it is not difficult to see why. There is a general feeling that poverty and all its concomitants are bad, and that there is an urgent need to do much more about them. Thus the inclination to couple terrorism and poverty, and the belief that aid to the less fortunate is in the long term the best, perhaps the only, effective solution for the terrorism problem.

Reducing poverty in the Third World is a moral as well as a political and economic imperative, but to expect from it a decisive change in the near future as far as terrorism is concerned is unrealistic, to say the least.

The link between terrorism and nationalist, ethnic, religious, and tribal conflict is far more tangible. These are many and need not be enumerated in detail. Solving these conflicts would probably bring about a certain reduction in the incidence of terrorism, but the conflicts are many, and if some of them have been defused in recent years, others have emerged. Nor are the issues clear-cut or the bones of contention easy to define, let alone to solve.

If the issue at stake is a certain territory or the demand for autonomy, a compromise through negotiations might be achieved, but it ought to be recalled that Al Qaeda was founded and September 11 occurred not because of a territorial dispute or the feeling of national oppression but because of a religious commandment—jihad and the establishment of shari'ah. Terrorist attacks in Central Asia and Morocco, in Saudi Arabia, Algeria, and partly in Iraq were mostly directed against fellow Muslims, not against infidels. Although appeasement may work in individual cases, terrorist groups with global ambitions cannot be appeased by territorial concessions.

As in the war against poverty, initiatives to solve local conflicts are overdue and should be welcomed, but there should be no illusions with regard to the wider effect of a peaceful solution of one conflict or another. To give one obvious example: peace (or at least the absence of war) between Israel and the Palestinians would be a blessing for those concerned, but the assumption that the resolution of a local conflict (even one of great symbolic importance) would have a dramatic effect in other parts of the world is unfounded. Osama bin Laden did not go to war because of Gaza and Nablus; he did not send his warriors to fight in Palestine. Even the disappearance of the "Zionist entity" would not have a significant impact on his supporters, except perhaps to provide encouragement for further action.

Such a warning against illusions is called for because there is a great deal of wishful thinking and naiveté around this issue: if only there were peace between Israelis and Palestinians, all the other conflicts would be manageable. But the problems are as much in Europe, Asia, and Africa as in the Middle East; there is a great deal of aggression that could (and probably would) easily turn in other directions once one conflict has been defused.

It seems likely, for instance, that in the years to come the struggle against the "near enemy" (the governments of the Arab and some non-Arab Muslim countries) will again feature prominently. There has been for some time a truce among Al Qaeda and related groups, partly for strategic reasons (to concentrate on the tight against America and the West) and partly because attacks against fellow Muslims, even apostates, are bound to be less popular than fighting the infidels. But this truce, as events in Saudi Arabia and elsewhere show, may be coming to an end.

Tackling the supposed sources of terrorism, even for the wrong reasons, will do no harm and may bring some good, but it does not bring us any nearer to an understanding of the real sources of terrorism, a field that has become a circus ground for riding hobby-horses and peddling preconceived notions.

* * *

At the present time almost all attention is focused on Islamist terrorism, but it is useful to remember that this was not always the case—even as recently as thirty years ago—and that there are a great many conflicts and perceived oppressions that may come to the fore in the years ahead. Indeed, these need not even be major conflicts now that small groups have access to weapons of mass destruction.

Islamist terrorism certainly has not yet run its course, but it is unlikely that the present fanaticism will last forever. Religious-nationalist fervor does not constantly burn with the same intensity. There is a phenomenon known in Egypt as "Salafi burnout," the mellowing of radical young people, the weakening of the original fanatical impetus. Like all other movements in history, messianic groups are subject to routinization, to the circulation of generations, and to changing political circumstances. This could happen as a result of either victories or defeats. One day, it might be possible to appease militant Islamism—though hardly in the current period of burning aggression, when faith in global victory has not yet been broken.

Some leading students of Islam have argued that radical Islamism passed its prime years ago and that its downfall and disappearance are only a question of time, perhaps not much time. It is true that societies that were exposed to the rule of fundamentalist fanatics (such as Iran) or to radical Islamist attacks (such as Algeria) have been immunized to a certain extent. Some fanatics, however, can always he found, and as these lines are written, volunteers for suicide missions are being enlisted in cities across Iran and Algeria. In any case, many countries have not yet undergone such first-hand experience; for them the rule of shari'ah and the restoration of the caliphate are still brilliant dreams. By and large, then, the predictions about the imminent demise of Islamism have been premature, while no doubt correct in the long run.

In the short term, however, the danger remains acute and may, in fact, grow. Terrorist attacks will not necessarily be directed against the greatest and most dangerous enemy as perceived by the terrorist gurus. Much depends on where terrorists are strong and where they believe the enemy to be weak. That terrorist attacks are likely to continue in the Middle East goes without saying; other danger zones are Central Asia and, above all, Pakistan.

Western Europe has become, over a number of years, a major base for terrorist support groups, a process that has been facilitated by the growth of Muslim communities, the growing tensions with native populations, and the ease with which radicals can organize in certain mosques and cultural organizations. Indoctrination is provided by militants who come to these countries as religious dignitaries. This freedom of action is considerably greater than that enjoyed in the Arab and Muslim world. True, there have been some arrests and closer controls after September 11, but given the legal and political restrictions under which the European security services labor, effective counteraction is still exceedingly difficult.

European governments frequently have been criticized for not having done enough to integrate Muslim newcomers into their societies, but integration was usually not what the new-comers wanted. They wanted to preserve their religious and ethnic identity and their way of life, and they resented intervention by secular authorities. The great majority of first-generation immigrants wanted to live in peace and quiet and to make a living for their families, but they have little control over their offspring.

The radicalization of the second generation of immigrants is a common phenomenon all over the world. This generation has often been only superficially acculturated and feels resentment and hostility more acutely. Feelings of exclusion, sexual repression (a taboo subject in this context), and other factors have led to aggression and ultimately to crime directed against their neighbors and the authorities.

True, the number of extremists is small. Among British Muslims, for instance, only 13 percent have expressed sympathy and support for terrorist attacks, but this still amounts to about 200,000, far more than needed for staging a terrorist campaign. The figure is suspect in any case because not all of those sharing radical views will openly express them to strangers.

But, again, prospects are less hopeless in the long term. The temptations of Western civilization are corrosive; young Muslims cannot he kept in hermetically sealed ghettos. They may be disgusted and repelled by alcohol, loose morals, general decadence, and all the other evils of the society they inhabit, but they are at the same time fascinated and attracted by them. This is hound to affect their activist fervor, and they will he exposed not only to the negative aspects of the world surrounding them but also to its values. Other religions had to face these temptations over the ages and by and large have been fighting a losing battle.

It is often forgotten that only a relatively short period passed from the beginnings of Islam in the Arabian desert to the splendor and luxury (and learning and poetry) of Harun al-Rashid's Baghdad—from the austere Koran to the ribald Arabian Nights. The pulse of contemporary history is beating much faster, but is it beating fast enough? For it is a race against time. The advent of megaterrorism and the access to weapons of mass destruction are dangerous enough, but coupled with fanaticism they generate scenarios too unpleasant to contemplate.

There can be no final victory in the fight against terrorism, for terrorism is the contemporary manifestation of conflict, and conflict will not disappear from the earth until human nature undergoes a basic change. But it is in our power to make life for terrorists and potential terrorists much more difficult.

It is often argued that terrorism cannot be defeated by weapons alone but requires a struggle for hearts and minds, a confrontation of ideas (or ideologies). If it were only that easy. Each case is different, and many terrorist groups do not have any specific idea or ideology, but instead have a fervent belief, of either a religious or a political nature. They fight for demands, territorial or otherwise, that seem to them self-evident, and they want to defeat their enemies. They are not open to dialogue or rational debate. When Mussolini was asked during the early days of fascism about his program concerning the socialists, he said that his program was to smash their skulls.

The why-do-they-hate-us question is often raised in this context, along with the question of what can be done about it—that is, making use of soft power in combating terrorism. Disturbing figures have been published about the low (and decreasing) popularity of America in foreign parts. Yet it is too often forgotten that international relations is not a popularity contest and that big and powerful countries have always been feared, resented, and envied. This has been the case since the days of the Assyrians and the Roman Empire. Neither the Ottoman nor the Spanish Empire, the Chinese, the Russian, nor the Japanese empires were ever popular. British sports were emulated in the colonies, and French culture impressed the local elites in North Africa and Indochina, but this did not lead to political support, let alone identification with the rulers.

A moderate and intelligent policy on the part of the great power, concessions, and good deeds may mitigate somewhat the perceived threat but cannot remove it, because great powers remain potentially dangerous. They could always change their policies and become nasty, arrogant, and aggressive.

Life could he made more difficult for terrorists by imposing more controls and restrictions wherever useful. But neither the rules of national or international law are adequate to deal with terrorism. Many terrorists or suspected terrorists have been detained in America and in Europe, but only a handful have been put on trial and convicted, because inadmissible evidence was submitted or the authorities were reluctant to reveal the sources of their information and thus lose those sources. As a result, many who were almost certainly involved in terrorist operations were never arrested, while others were acquitted or simply released from detention.

* * *

It could well be that, as far as the recent past is concerned, the danger of terrorism has been overstated. In the two world wars, more people were killed and more material damage was caused in a few hours than through all the terrorist attacks of recent years. The real issue is the coming danger. Megaterrorism has not yet arrived; even 9/11 was a stage between old-fashioned terrorism and the shape of things to come: the use of weapons of mass destruction.

That such weapons will be used is a real possibility. For the first time in human history very small groups have the power to cause immense destruction. Political solutions to deal with their grievances may sometimes be possible but this will frequently not he the case. Today's terrorists, in their majority, are not diplomats eager to negotiate or to find compromises. And even if some would he satisfied with less than total victory and the annihilation of the enemy, there will always be a more radical group eager to continue the struggle.

Perhaps this scenario is too pessimistic; perhaps the weapons of mass destruction, for whatever reason, will never be used. But it would he the first time in human history that a lethal weapon, once invented, went unused. In the last resort, the problem is, of course, the human condition. In 1932, when Einstein attempted to induce Freud to support pacifism, Freud replied that there was no likelihood of suppressing humanity's aggressive tendencies. If there were any reason for hope, it was that people would turn away on rational grounds, realizing that war had become too destructive.

Freud was partly correct: war (at least between great powers) has become far less likely for rational reasons. But his argument does not apply to terrorism motivated not by political or economic interests but based on fanaticism with an admixture of madness. Terrorism, therefore, will continue—not perhaps with the same intensity at all times, and some parts of the globe may he spared altogether. But there can he no victory, only an uphill struggle, at times successful, at other times not.

Walter Laqueur is the co-chair of the International Research Council at the Center for Strategic and International Studies, Washington. He recently published *No End to War* (2004).

Also available from Gibson Square

HOUSE OF BUSH HOUSE OF SAUD
by Craig Unger

*Uncovering the secret 30-year relationship of
the Bush family and Iraq's neighbour,
Saudi Arabia.*

'Leaves the reader more than a little disturbed.'
Guardian
Book of the Week

'A notably intelligent piece of investigative reporting.'
Observer